"Are we Tax Slaves of a Lower Order than those Lying EDOMITES?"

(HOW to be Liberated from all Slavery, Worldwide!)

By
The Worldwide People's Revolution!®

Book 052 ♥ ✳ ✡

(The Cover Photo shows Work Slaves, Tax Slaves, Insurance Slaves, Interest/Usury Slaves, Drug Slaves, Food Bills Slaves, Rent Slaves, Transportation Slaves, Repair Bills Slaves, Heating and Cooling Bills Slaves, ElecTrickery Bills Slaves, Gas Bills Slaves, Water Bills Slaves, Telephone Bills Slaves, Entertainment Bills Slaves, Childcare Slaves, and Various other Kinds of SLAVES: beCause most of the People in this World of Woes are Slaves of the Edomites, who are also Slaves of Various Kinds; but, being Materially and Financially Rich, they do not Care about it! However, the very Poor Slaves most Certainly do Care about it: beCause they must Suffer for it!)

Copyright, Dedication and Introduction

By our Selected King's Chief Editor,
Dr. Samuel Walker Edison, Ph.D., MA, BS and QC!

ISBN — 13: 978-1720-3333-64
ISBN — 10: 1720-33336X

00-01 [_] God Forbid that our Selected King should Abuse his Artistic / Literary License, and Impersonate any Infamous Characters of the Past — such as that Wicked Adolf Hitler and Saint Joseph Stalin, whom **"The Divided States of United Lies"** Supported during the Second World War, whose Friendly Bankers Gained hundreds of Billions of Dollars by Supporting both Sides of that HATEFUL War: beCause it was very Profitable for them — beCause, by Abusing his Literary License, he might be Banned from Publishing any and even all of his Inspired Books, Worldwide: beCause the EDOMITES Control the World, and in many more Ways than one or 2: beCause it is in their Greater FINANCIAL Interests to make themselves Excessively RICH, which can easily be Proven in a Courtroom with Law and Order, with a Riichus Juj in Charge of it, which is the Last Place that a True Red, White and Blue-blooded Edomite Wants to Discover himself: beCause he just Naturally HATES the Bright Shining Light of Provable Truths; and neither will he come into that Light, lest his Evil Deeds should be Exposed and Reproved, even as Jesus Christ pointed out in *John 3:19—21:*

> *"And this is the Condemnation, that Bright Lights and Marvelous Truths have come into this World of Woes; but, Evil Men Loved the Darkness of Ignorance, rather than the Light of Truths: because their Words and Deeds were Evil. Indeed, everyone who does Evil, Hates the Light of Provable Truths, neither comes to the Light, lest his Evil Deeds should be Reproved; but, he who does Good Works and Speaks the Truth, Cheerfully comes into the Light: so that his Words and Deeds might be made Known — that they are Worked According to the Will of God, who is a Lover of all Provable Truths, which alone can Liberate Ignorant People, who are Tormented Slaves of an Evil Empire."* — The New MAGNIFIED Version (NMV) in Plain English for Honest Wise People.

00-02 [_] Therefore, this Inspired Book is COPYRIGHTED AD 2018—20,000,018 by **The Worldwide People's Revolution!®** All Rights are Reserved for the Truth's Sake. No Portion of this Unique Book shall be Reproduced by any Means for Sale without Written Permission from **The Worldwide People's Revolution!®** However, everyone in the World has the Right to Reproduce Exact Copies of this Inspired Book, and Sell them for a Reasonable Profit, and KEEP 90 percent of the Net Profits for their own Prosperity: beCause our Selected King only wants 10% of the Net Profits for the Construction of **"The Great World TEMPLE of PEACE!"** (**The Glory of Jerusalem Arises Again!**) By The Worldwide People's Revolution!® Book 017.

00-03 [_] O Doctor Samuel Walker Edison, it is a Literary SIN for anyone to make up their own Imaginary Version of the *Holy Bible,* which is the Infallible Pure Word of the Living God, who is the SAME — both Yesterday, Today and Forever: beCause he is the Unchangeable God from all of Eternity to all of Eternity, who never once Changed his Mind about anything, even though Jesus said: *"You have Heard that it has been said, 'You shall not Murder'; but, I now say to you that whosoever Hates his Brother without a Justified Cause is a Murderer within his Heart, and shall thus be Judged by God as a Murderer: beCause he has Condemned his Brother without any*

(HOW to be Liberated from all Slavery, Worldwide!)

Justified Causes. Therefore, he who Judges Rashly shall be Judged Rashly: beCause everyone Reaps whatever he or she Sows; and as you Measure out your Judgments on others, so shall you be Judged According to your own Words: beCause there is no other Fair nor Just Way to Do it, whereby True Justice can be Served to all Peoples. Therefore, if you Speak, be Sure to Speak as the Oracles of God, himself, who would only Speak the Truth, the Whole Truth, and nothing but the Whole Truth: beCause he is a Lover of All that is GOOD, while the Devil is a Lover of All that is EVIL, whose Adopted Children are Spiritual COWARDS, who are Afraid of the Light of Truths, who Refuse to Answer your Most Important Questions, who are Terrified by Provable Truths: beCause they have been Living in a Manmade Delusion, and Specifically in a Manmade RELIGIOUS Delusion, whereby each False Religious Group Vainly Imagines that it Serves the One and ONLY True God — no matter who that God might be, nor what his Name might be: beCause he is THEIR God, and mostly an Invention of their own Deceived Minds, who have Strange Doctrines, who Believe in Insanity Clauses and Easter Bunnies laying Chocolate Eggs under Flowering Plastic Bushes for Innocent Children to Discover while being Blindfolded with Religious and Economic Hypocrisies, who have no Idea what the True Creator God Requires of People, whereby they might be Adopted into his Holy Family, if they Qualify. Yes, they must Pass their Spiritual Tests during this Life, or else be Born Again in some more Hellish Situation or Evil Condition, whereby they can be Tormented both Day and Night, until they come to their Right Senses with the Prodigal Son of Luke 15, and thus Confess all of their Sins, and thus Forsake their Sins, and thus Escape from their Prison of Lies and Religious Delusions." — The New MAGNIFIED Version of the Gospel According to Saint Bartholomew 39:47—53. †§‡§§

00-04 [_] Well, my Friend, in a Vain Attempt to Prove our Selected King to be WRong, you have only Proven him to be Correct: beCause his New MAGNIFIED Version is Inspired by the Holy Spirit. Therefore, this Special Book is now DEDICATED to Ignorant People like you, who have gotten their Wires Crossed, whereby they have Shorted themselves Out, and have Broken their Breakers, you might say, whereby their Lights have gone Out; and thus they Walk in the Darkness of Ignorance with those Ancient Scribes and Pharisees, who clearly said to Jesus: *"We have Moses and the Holy Prophets for Good Guides; and therefore, we do not Need nor Want to Hear any of your Outlandish Lies."* Yes, they said: *"We have Heard him [Stephen] say that that Jesus of Nazareth shall Destroy this Place, and shall Change the Customs that Moses Delivered to us, who alone can be Trusted: because God Spoke to him, Face to Face, even as a Man Speaks with another Man; and yet he did not Die, in spite of the Fact that God said that no Man could See his Face, lest that Man should Die for it."* {See *John 5:45—46; 7:19; Acts 6:14; Romans 10:4; Hebrews 7:12; Genesis 32:30; Exodus 33:11, and Verses 20—23, King James Version (KJV),* for a Major Contradiction within that *"Holy Bible."*}

00-05 [_] O Dr. Edison, I like *Hebrews 9:22,* which Clearly States: *"And According to the Laws of Moses, almost all Things are Purged or Cleansed by Means of Blood; and without the Shedding of Blood, there is no Remission or Forgiveness of Sins."* Indeed, that is why it is Important that the Israelis get into a World War with Iran, whereby enough Blood can be Shed to Cleanse the Middle East from Ancient Jewish Myths — such as that Non-Biblical Nonsense about People going to Heaven when they Die, when both God and his Chosen Son, Jesus Christ, Know for a Fact that no one is going to Heaven when he or she Dies, except for Jesus, himself, who alone Qualified for such a State of Glory. (See *John 3:13, KJV.*) Therefore, **"The Divided States of United Lies"** should do its Best to Help those Deceived Israelis get into that Great War, just to Fulfill Prophecies in *the Book of Revelation* — one of which Calls for the Battle of

(HOW to be Liberated from all Slavery, Worldwide!)

Armageddon, whereby the Blood will be running as High as the Bridles on the Horses, or about 3 Feet Deep, a Mile Wide and 200 Miles Long: beCause it is Necessary to Cleanse the Minds of those Bloodthirsty Edomites, who LOVE those Hateful Gory Wars! Otherwise, they would Cheerfully Submit to **"The Swanky Sword of Divine Truths!" (The Most Powerful Weapon in the Whole Universe!) By The Worldwide People's Revolution!®** Book 067. †§‡

00-06 [_] Well, my Friend, this Inspired Book Reveals HOW to Prevent any and all such Hateful Bloody Wars, if anyone is Interested in **"Guaranteed Solutions!" (HOW to Solve our Local and Global Problems in the Most Rational Manner Possible!) By The Worldwide People's Revolution!®** Book 080.

00-07 [_] O Doctor Sam, are you saying that all of those Prophecies within *the Book of Revelation* were given on CONDITIONS? For Example, if People Humble themselves by Means of Fasting and Praying, until they become Like Innocent Children with Pure Minds and Clean Bodies, will God not have Mercy on them and Forgive them, and thus Turn Away his Fierce Wrath from them, and even Heal the Land, and Restore every Truth that has been Lost, whereby we might be Saved from the Destructions to Come?

00-08 [_] Yes, that is Exactly what I am Saying: beCause it was Revealed to our Selected King, Years Ago, who Wrote more than 300 Exceptionally Good Books by the Gift of Inspiration from God. Therefore, we would do Well to Study them, and not be Lazy about it: beCause there is no Need for the Battle of Armageddon, if we all Repent. However, if the Masses of People Reject the Great Truths that he has Taught, that will be their Just Reward.

00-09 [_] O Doctor Sam, I Promise to Carefully Read ALL of this Book, since it is so Short.

00-10 [_] Well, if anyone Agrees with that Statement, they should Check the Box with an X.

Explanations for Symbols:

† This Dagger is called "The Sword of Controversy," which Means that someone Disagrees with the Statement, which could include the Author, himself.

‡ This Double Dagger is called "The Double-edged Sword of Controversies," which Means that the Issue must be Settled at: **"The Great Worldwide TELEVISED Court HEARING!" (That Great Meeting of the Most Intelligent and Well-Educated Minds!) By The Worldwide People's Revolution!®** Book 041.

§ This Section Symbol represents Sarcastic Statements, which likely Mean the Opposite of what is Written. Two such Symbols (§§) together, Means that the Statement is so Sarcastic that it Proves itself to be WRong. For Example, the Edomites are Holy People, like Father Abraham, who told the Palestinians that if they Chose the Best Land in Israel, they could have it, and also have Jerusalem as their International Capital for all Honest Nations of Wise People to Inherit, who will Establish **"The New RIGHTEOUS One-World Government!" (HOW to Establish a Righteous One-World Government without Going to WAR!) By The Worldwide People's Revolution!®** Book 056. †§‡§§

🔔 The Bell follows Statements that should be Memorized.
This Inspired Book contains 3 Black and White Photographs and about 59,000 Words.

The Fascinating Menu on the Table of Contents

Chapter 01 — WHO are the Edomites? ... 7

Chapter 02 — HOW to Live Well without Bankers! ... 9

Chapter 03 — Will the Edomites be Infuriated by this Plan? ... 13

Chapter 04 — Why do the Edomites Think of us Tax Slaves as Beasts? ... 16

Chapter 05 — The Original Book, Slightly Modified to Fit the Times! ... 20

Chapter 06 — Adolf Hitler Junior takes up his Unholy Mutilated Bible! ... 34

Chapter 07 — The Greatest Sin is the Rejection of Truths! ... 38

Chapter 08 — HOW to get an Instant Army of Working Soldiers! ... 41

Chapter 09 — "Give to me LIBERTY, or Give to me DEATH!" ... 43

Chapter 10 — "Are we Tax Slaves of a Lower Order than those Lying EDOMITES?" ... 48

Chapter 11 — The Mark of the Beast is the Best Solution! ... 54

Chapter 12 — Freedom Comes at Last! ... 56

Chapter 13 — It is now High Time for Someone to be in Charge! ... 62

Chapter 14 — Eternally Good Money without Inflation! ... 66

Chapter 15 — Bullies will not be in Charge! ... 70

Chapter 16 — Countless Books for Sale! ... 72

Chapter 17 — Will the Lying Edomites Slip Through the Net that is Spread Out for them? ... 76

Chapter 18 — ORDER in the COURT! ... 80

Chapter 19 — Honest White Israelites will Triumph! ... 88

Chapter 20 — The Conclusion ... 91

Chapter 21 — Appendix — An E-mail Letter to Saint John McArdle of C-SPAN Fame ... 93

Chapter 22 — A List of other Fascinating Literature by the same Inspired Author ... 97

(HOW to be Liberated from all Slavery, Worldwide!)

— Chapter 01 —

WHO are the Edomites?

01-01 [_] *"I have Loved you, O Israel, says the Supreme Ruler. Yet you say, Wherein have you Loved us? Well, was Esau not Jacob's own Brother? — says the Supreme Ruler — yet I Loved Jacob, and I Hated Esau, and laid his Mountains and his Heritage a Wasteland for the Dragons and Snakes of the Wilderness to Inherit." — NMV of Malachi 1:2—3. "And Esau Hated his Brother Jacob: beCause of the Blessings wherewith his Father Isaac had Blest him; and Esau said within his Heart, 'The Days of Mourning for my Father Isaac are at Hand, and then I will Slay my Brother Jacob.' But, God Loved Jacob for his Goodness: beCause he was an Honest Hardworking Generous Person, even like his Fathers Isaac and Abraham." — NMV of Genesis 27:41. "As it is written, Jacob have I loved, but Esau have I hated." — KJV of Romans 9:13.*

01-02 [_] O Selected King of **The Worldwide People's Revolution!®**, are you Suggesting that you Believe any or perhaps even all of that Biblical Nonsense? Are you not Aware that the Edomites Died Out, along with at least 10 of the 12 Tribes of Israel, who perhaps never even Existed: beCause the entire Bible is nothing but Jewish Mythology? †§‡

01-03 [_] Well, my Friend, if the Hairy Intellectual Edomites, who are the Descendants of Esau, Died Out, why are they now in Control of all Major Banks, Medical Institutions, Drug Industries, Chemical Corporations, Weapons Manufacturing, Oil Industries, Hollywood Movie Productions, Book Publishing, and the News Media at large? Yes, it can easily be Proven in a Courtroom with Law and Order, and without going to War over it. *"Seek the Truth, and you shall Find it."* †‡

01-04 [_] O Selected King, with your Age and Life Experiences, you should Know by now that People cannot Rightly be put into Labeled Boxes, as if they had Established Values within each Box. For Example, not all Jews are Liars nor Betrayers of Trust, like Bernie Madoff and Judas Iscariot; but, some are Actually Honest Hardworking People, like yourself, who are known as White Jews, while the Liars and Deceivers are known as Red Jews — such as the Red-faced Communist Jews of the Union of Soviet Socialist Republicans (USSR), who made a Desperate Attempt to Upgrade the Living Standards of hundreds of millions of Poor People in that Part of the World, who were Living in Mud Huts, previous to the Communist Revolution, while the Rich Aristocrats were Living in Palaces with Gold Trimmings, and Eating from Silver Plates, and Drinking from Silver Cups — not that they did not Deserve it; but, that everyone from the Lowest Cockroach in the City Dump to the Zrr, himself, did Deserve it; but, the Economic System of Russian Communism did not Function Properly for Providing a High Standard of Living for so many People, which Required Capitalism to Rescue those Masses of People, after Communism Proved itself to be a FALSE Economic System. Yes, that is WHY there are now more than 20 Million Homeless Russians, and 10 Million Homeless Americans, or about as many as the entire Population of Cuba, which gives to us the Right to Mock the Cubans: beCause we are Chief Hypocritical Hypocritters. Indeed, we would have a Right to Criticize the Cubans, if they just had 1% as many Homeless and Near-Homeless People as we have; but, they have Zero Homeless People: beCause they are COMMUNISTS! And that Explains WHY God Hates those Wicked Edomites: beCause they Disregard the Glories of Demon-ocracy and its Economic Savior called Capitalism, which is a Christian Doctrine, straight out of *the Book of ACTS*, Chapters 4 and 5. Indeed, Jesus said that we should Love our Naaberz as much as we Love ourselves, which is WHY that I Sell Tobacco Products: beCause I Want everyone to get Equally as Addicted to Nicotine as I am, and I am NOT Crazy; but, I am Working on Driving myself Insane by Clinging Tightly to ALL that is GOOD, which is WHY that I Smoke those Stinking Cigarettes: beCause Lung Cancers give Medical Doctors and Drug Companies more Business. For Example, we Americans have Wasted more than a Trillion Dollars on Cancer Researches, only to Prove to God that we are the Good People. †§‡§§

01-05 [_] Well, my Potential Friend, before you Drive yourself Totally Insane, and become Like one of the Maggots of this World, you should at least Attempt to THINK, and Remember that there is a Great Day of Righteous Judgments coming, when all so-called "Secrets" will be Revealed, including those of the Lying Edomites, who are not Mentioned by the Snooze News Reporters, whereby you and many others have come to Sincerely Believe that the Edomites are EXTINCT! †§‡

01-06 [_] So, O Selected King, if the Edomites are NOT Extinct, WHERE are they Hiding themselves among us?

01-07 [_] They are "Hiding" in Plain Sight, even as they have done for thousands of Years, which is also True of the Lost 10 Tribes of the Israelites, who are easily Identified by their Good Works, even as the Edomites are easily Identified by their Sour Fruits, which are EVIL — such as the Production and Sales of Hateful Military Weapons, whereby they have Raked in no less than 10 Trillion Dollars for their "Services." However, no Clan on the Earth has Profited more than those Friendly High-ranking Banksters, who have Raked in no less than 100 Trillion Dollars for their "Services," and mostly from the Interest Slaves of **"The Divided States of United Lies!" (The so-called "United States of North America" in Disguise!) By The Worldwide People's Revolution!®** Book 058.

01-08 [_] O Selected King of **The Worldwide People's Revolution!®**, are you Suggesting that we Education Slaves, Work Slaves, Tax Slaves, Insurance Slaves, Interest Slaves, Rent Slaves, and Endless Bills Slaves could Live Healthy Happy Lives without the Assistance of BANKERS? Have you Lost your RIIT Miind? Even Jesus Christ Believed in the Goodness of Bankers. (See *Luke 19:23, KJV*.) Therefore, we can Thank God for all such Good People: because we could not Live Well without them. †§‡

01-09 [_] Well, my Potential Friend, it is most Obvious that you have not Studied a Wonderful Book, called: **"SWANGKEENOMIKS Rules the Roost!" (HOW all People can Prosper in a RIIT WAA, and STOP Polluting the Earth with Capitalist TRASH!)**, Book 039, which is a Companion Book of: **"Poverty Hunger Riots Strikes Brutalities Election Deceptions and Civil Wars!" (The High Price that we Earthlings have Paid for Leaving the Good Land!)**, Book 014, which is a Companion Book of: **"Are Americans the Most STUPID People who ever Lived?" (HOW Working People can PROSPER and Live in PEACE Under the Rulership of a RIGHTEOUS KING!) By The Worldwide People's Revolution!®** Book 047.

01-10 [_] O Elected King of the Highest Mountains of Good Understanding, I have Carefully "Red" all of those Inspired Books, and I Know for a Fact that we Americans Fulfill that Prophecy in *Revelation 3:17* — *"Because you say, I am Rich and Increased with Goods, and have Need of Nothing; but, you know not that you are Extremely Poor, Blind, Wretched, Miserable and Stark Naked in the Light of Provable Truths ..."*

— Chapter 02 —

HOW to Live Well without Bankers!

02-01 [_] Now, we Know for a Fact that Moses, Joshua, King David, Solomon, and all of the other Kings of Israel Lived Well without the Assistance of any Bankers, since they did not Mention them in any of their Good Books. However, the Edomites did Establish Banks and Bankers several hundred Years before Christ: beCause they soon Discovered the Great Advantages for Loaning Money and Collecting Usury on all such Loans, which Moses Forbid in *Exodus 22:25 and Leviticus 25:36—37*, stating:

> *"If you Lend Money to any one of my People, who is Living Poorly beside you, you shall not be to him as an Usurer, or Collector of Interest on Loans; neither shall you lay upon him any other Kind of Usury: because his Burdens are already far too Great to Bear; but, you shall do for him as you would Want some Rich Person to do for you, if you were Extremely Poor, and had to Borrow Money or Tools, just to Survive. You shall not Collect any Usury from him, nor any Increase of any Kind; but, you shall Fear your God, so that your Poor Brother may Live with you in Peace, and also Prosper by his own Labors. Therefore, you shall not give to him your Money upon Usury, nor shall you Lend to him your Foods nor Tools for any Increase: because it is a Sin in my Eyesight."*

Therefore, when the Edomites Learned about that Statute, which presented a Greater Temptation than the Forbidden Fruit in the Garden of Eden, they Quickly Adopted that Idea of Charging Usury on Loans, and then ran with it to several other Ancient Kingdoms, including those of Egypt, Babylon, Persia (Iran), Greece and Rome: beCause of the Convenience of Exchanging Goods and Services by Using Money, which was normally made of Minted Coins with Numbers and Figures on them, which had Set Values, which remained Consistent for thousands of Years. For Example, a Pair of Shoes in the Land of Israel Costed the same at about the Time of Christ as they Costed at about the Time of Father Abraham, who Lived about 2,000 Years before Christ: beCause the Israelites did not Surrender their Government Rights to the Edomites, until about the Time of Christ, when the Edomites got themselves into Control of the Government and the Temple, and the so-called "Holy Books," which their Fathers had already Corrupted with Edomite Myths, whereby they became the Enemies of Jesus Christ and his Self-Disciplined Disciples, who Practiced the Love of God, who is All that is GOOD. ‡

02-02 [_] O Selected King of **The Worldwide People's Revolution!®**, are you Suggesting that the Edomites Infiltrated the Kingdoms of Babylon and Persia, and Persuaded them to Adopt the

Edomite Financial Plan, which is to Loan Money to Poor People for the Purpose of Collecting Interest or Usury from them, whereby they might Produce X-amount of Usury Slaves for themselves, who made themselves into Masters of Money Games, even as it is until this very Day? Are you saying that no such Money was even Needed by those Poor People?

02-03 [_] Well, if you Think about it with a Capital T, there was a Certain Need for a Righteous One-World GovernMINT, with Universal Money of only ONE Kind, which could be Used Wisely in all Nations, without Money Exchangers Exchanging any Moneys for Collecting more Usury for the Edomites, which Good GovernMINT simply Mints and Prints the Necessary New Money — NOT to Give it Away to Rich Bankers, nor to Poor Beggars; but, in Order to Use that New Money WISELY, in Order to HIRE whomever is Willing and Able to Learn and Work, in Order to Help Build those **"GLORIOUS Swanky Hotels Castles and Fortresses!" (Beautiful Planned City States for WISE Intelligent Well-Educated People with Common Sense and Good Understanding!) By The Worldwide People's Revolution!®** Book 019. ⚜ But, there was no Need for any Bankers, except to Store the Money that someone might Earn by Honest Labor, who might Need some SECURE Storage Place to Keep it, which could be Guarded by the Federal Government Soldiers, or by some Policemen or Security Guards, which could more easily be Guarded within a SECURE Swanky CASTLE. However, when the Edomites saw all of that Stored Money in the Banks, they easily Persuaded the Rulers to make Good Use of it by Loaning it to Poor People, whom they could make into their Interest Slaves FOREVER, just by Keeping them POOR on Minimum Wages! For Example, if some Poor Person should Borrow 100 Dollars / Shekels from a Friendly Banker, who Trusted him to Return it with Interest, he was Happy to do so: beCause he could Transform that Money into a lot more Money, just by Buying some Tools to Work with — such as Shoemaking Tools, whereby he could Produce a Necessary Product, and thus Earn an Honest Living, while that Friendly Banker would supposedly "Earn" his Money by making the Loan, which would not be the Case with a Righteous Government: beCause it would have no Desire nor Will to make any Usury Slaves of any People, even if they were Foreigners: beCause of Loving their Naaberz as much as they Love themselves, which is a True Christian Doctrine. ‡

02-04 [_] O Elected King, I Pray to God that you get **"The New RIGHTEOUS One-World Government"** Established as soon as Possible: beCause I am getting SICK of being an Interest Slave for my Friendly Banker, or Usury Master. For Example, I Borrowed 150,000 Dollars for the Purpose of Buying my Wooden / Firetrap House, about 40 Years Ago, whereby I have Bought that House no less than 4 Times by Way of Interest Payments, Property Taxes, Insurance, and Repair Bills! Yes, I was telling my Brother Tom about that, and he said with Shock: "That is Unbelievable! However, now that I Think about it, I have done the same Silly Thing; but, at least I got to Live in the Land of the FREE!" And I said, "But, just how FREE are People who are 20 Trillion Dollars in DEBT to those Edomites?" And he said, "And WHO are the Edomites?" And I said, "They are the Slave Masters." And he said, "And WHO are the Slaves?" And I said, "They are People like us, who get up each Workday and go to Work for our Slave Masters, who are also Tax Slaves, Insurance Slaves, Interest Slaves, and Endless Bills Slaves, just like we are: beCause they all Buy into the same Edomite LIE — that it is Impossible to Live without the Assistance of Bankers, unless you Want to Live in some Jungle, in Africa or in South America. Indeed, if you Want to have a Standard of Living above that of Wild Beasts, you have to Conform to the Established Economic System, which is Conveniently Arranged by the Edomites, for the Edomites and of the Edomites: beCause they are the Inventors of all such so-called 'Good Things' as the Bursting Housing Bubble Financial Plan, the Great Recessions, and the Great Depressions: beCause they Gain TRILLIONS of Dollars by Means of all such 'Good Things.' Therefore, do you now Understand that?" And he said, "Hmmm, I never Thought of it before now. However, I Promise to Think about it with a Capital T, until I come to Fully Understand it, whereby I might Teach it to my Children, Friends, Relatives and Naaberz."†

02-05 [_] Well, my Friend, we all Know for a Fact that your Story is NOT True: beCause no such Fictitious Conversation ever Occurred; but, the Truths in your Parable have Occurred on a Daily Basis for thousands of Years, which can easily be Proven in a Courtroom with Law and Order, without any Silly Arguments: beCause of having a Righteous JUDGE in Charge of it, who Keeps the Court in ORDER, who only Allows one Person to Speak at one Time: so that People are not Attempting to Shout over the Top of whomever is Speaking; but, everyone has a Right to Speak whatever Truths might be in his or her Mind, until the Issue is Settled. ‡

02-06 [_] O Selected King of **The Worldwide People's Revolution!®**, there is no Way on Earth that all such Opinions can be Presented within a whole Day: beCause the Court Hearing would have to be 10 Billion Hours Long! In Fact, if you Allowed my Aunt Wretched to get her Mouth in Gear, and Step on her Intellectual Accelerator — even as she often does on the *Washington Journal* on the C-SPAN Network — you could well Expect her to Run her Mouth in High Gear for a whole Hour, and only make a Point or 2, and never Mention any of the Great Truths that you Teach. {See www.amazon.com for: **"The Washington Journal is a FARCE!" (C-SPAN Managers are not very WISE!) By The Worldwide People's Revolution!®** Book 006.} †§‡

02-07 [_] Well, my Friend, what you are saying is True; but, only in such Open Forums as the *Washington Journal,* which Sorely Lacks ORDER. For Example, when we Hold **"The Great Worldwide TELEVISED Court HEARING,"** only the Sane People with Guaranteed Solutions will be Allowed to Speak, who have E-mailed their Messages to their Commanding Officers, who will Judge all such Messages, and then, if they Agree with them, they will E-mail those Messages to their Commanding Officers, until at last those Messages reach the Courtroom, which will Naturally Require some TIME; but, not half of Eternity, as it might Require on the *Washington Journal,* which has no Telephone Numbers for any Guaranteed Solutions for anything! In Fact, the Responses at that Great Meeting of the Most Intelligent Minds will mostly be by People who have what they Believe to be **"Guaranteed Solutions!"** (HOW to Solve our Local and Global Problems in the Most Rational Manner Possible!) By The Worldwide People's Revolution!® Book 080. Therefore, when some Commanding Officer makes a Fool of himself by Presenting some Childish Solution from one of his Sincere, but Deceived Servants, he will have to Step Down a Rank or 2: beCause of Misjudging the Contributed E-mail. Therefore, within Minutes, or even within Seconds, all of the other Commanding Officers will STOP and THINK, before they Present any such Foolish Statements in front of all of the Television Networks in the Whole World: beCause they will not Want to be Demoted by even so much as a Demerit. Indeed, they will all be less Bold about making any Foolish Statements in front of their Elected King, who will also be that Righteous Judge in Charge of the Court Hearings. ‡

02-08 [_] O Selected King of **The Worldwide People's Revolution!®**, that all Sounds like a Dictatorship to me. Indeed, everyone should be Free to Speak at one Time, even if no one can Hear anything that is Said, which is called DEMOCRACY, which is the only True Form of Good

Government, when it is an Established REPUBLIC, whereby Elected Officials, called CONgress People and SINators, get to VOTE concerning each Important Issue, which is Conglomerated into what Politicians call BILLS, along with no less than 2,000 other Issues, which are all Mixed Together like a Mud Pie by Legalistic Lawyers, which is then Thrown into the Faces of the Electors as a Democratic Republic! †§‡§§ ⌂

02-09 [_] Well, my Potential Friend, it is more Accurately called DEMON-ocracy, or MOB Rulership, which is Total Confusion and MADNESS in **"The BIG White OUTHOUSE on the Not-so-Biblical Capitol DUNGHILL,"** in Washington, District of Chief Criminals, which is easy to Prove by Watching and Listening to the *Washington Journal* on the C-SPAN Network. In Fact, it is a Rare Thing that any Intelligent Well-Educated People even Bother themselves to Call the *Washington Journal*: beCause they already Know that they are likely to be Cut Off by Pedro before they can Finish their Thoughts: because only Saint John McArdle and Steve Scully have enough Patience to Hear them Out, and only a Limited Amount of Time to Accept a few Calls. However, there could be 10,000 "Screeners," who Record and Judge the Worthiness of all such Calls to be Heard, and therefore get the Best of their Words into the *Washington Journal* — except that most of the Callers would Naturally be Pissed Off by it: beCause their Voices would not be Heard in a Democratic Forum, as in a Town Meeting at the City Hall Auditorium, which should Accommodate all of the Qualified Adult People within the City, who have Filled Out and Filed in the Courthouse **"The Complete SURVEYS of our VALUES!" (SURVEYS of Religious Spiritual Political Governmental Sexual Social Moral Economic Business Labor Habitual and Miscellaneous VALUES!) By The Worldwide People's Revolution!®**, Book 059, which might also Explain WHY there are Normally only a Dozen or so CONgress People in the House of Representatives during any given Workday, from Tuesday to Thursday afternoon, for a Total of about 1,200 Hours per Year, whose Speaker of the House only shows his Face for 2 to 3 Minutes, and then Disappears: beCause he Obviously does not Want to Hear what the Opposition Party has to Say — all of whom Address their Speeches to HIM, none of whom have ever Presented any of the Great Truths that I have now Presented to you. †‡ {See: **"Our Elected King Who Speaks Out!" (It is High Time for some Sane Person to Get Control of this Insane World!) By The Worldwide People's Revolution!®** Book 070.}

02-10 [_] O Selected King, that is the Beauty of **"FREEDUM uv SPEECH!" (U Speshoul Maguzeen uv Onist Upinyunz!) By The Worldwide People's Revolution!®** Book 030-0001. Indeed, everyone is Welcome to Contribute whatever Honest Opinions that they might have, which will be Read, Judged, Graded, and Posted by **"The New RIGHTEOUS One-World Government,"** somewhere within a Future Magazine of Honest Opinions, which will be Published for Free on the Internet, and in all Major Languages for whomever might Want to Study those Opinions. Therefore, that is the Best Solution known to Mankind, which is just another one of your Great Ideas; but, nothing like those **"GLORIOUS Swanky Hotels Castles and Fortresses,"** which will Solve no less than 5,000 Minor and Major Problems in this World of Woes — such as Air Pollution, Water Pollution, Trash Dump Insanity, Climate Changes, Vehicular Accidents, Drug Trafficking, Sex Trafficking, Needless Taxes, Police DEPARTments, Fire DEPARTments, Homeland Security Nonsense, Terrorist Attacks, and all Kinds of SLAVERY! Yes, one must Study your Master Plan, Carefully, just to See the Vision of it all; but, once one does See the Vision, there is no Way to Extract it from his nor her Mind: beCause there are ZERO Disadvantages for Building and Living in all such Beautiful Planned City States!

In Fact, it is now Possible and most Practical to Bless every Honest Hardworking Person in the Whole World, by using Mechanical Slaves to make **"Beautiful Swanky PALACES!" (A New Concept in Living Habits — Swanky Palaces for Poor People!) By The Worldwide People's Revolution!® Book 066.** †‡

— Chapter 03 —

Will the Edomites be Infuriated by this Plan?

03-01 [_] Well, if you were one of those so-called "Rich Edomites," who does not even have Fresh Clean Air to Breathe, Pure Living Water to Drink, Wholesome Natural Foods to Eat, Natural Clothing to Wear, nor a Secure Swanky Stone Dome Home Complex to Live within, behind the THICK Protective Stone Walls of a First Class Swanky FORTRESS, you would just Naturally be Worried about all such Inspired Words of Provable Truths: beCause it would be Possible for your Babylonian Empire to FALL within just ONE Hour, as *the Book of Revelation* puts it: beCause this is the Freedom of Speech Generation, which can easily Send a HOT Message all around the World within Seconds! Therefore, an Inspired Book like this one can "Travel" quite Rapidly on the Wings of Modern Communications, if anyone is Interested in True Freedom with a Capital T and F, even as they should all be: beCause they could all have a very Bright and Optimistic Future, if they had the Faith of a Mustard Seed. {See www.Amazon.com for: **"The Seven Basic Spiritual Building Blocks of LIFE!" (Faith Hope Trust Love Patience Persistence and Obedience!) By The Worldwide People's Revolution!® Book 036.**}

03-02 [_] O Elected King of **"The New RIGHTEOUS One-World Government,"** I am Amazed that we have not Heard the Truth about all of those Things a Long Time Ago. Indeed, how could it take 6,000+ Years to Learn about such a Good Government, which has an Unlimited Supply of New Money, which must be EARNED by Honest Labor, according to: **"A List of FAIR Swanky Wages!" (The Equitable Wage System!) By The Worldwide People's Revolution!® Book 065?**

03-03 [_] Well, my New Friend, it took that Long: beCause those Edomites Underhandedly Removed those Truths from the *"Holy Bible"* about such a Good Government before the Time of Christ, whom they Crucified for Revealing those same Truths during his Life, which you can easily Discover within **"The New MAGNIFIED Version of the GOOD NEWS According to Saint LUKE!" (The Magnified Gospel of Luke in Plain English!)**, Book 061, which is a Companion Book of: **"The New MAGNIFIED Version of the Book of ACTS!" (The Understandable Version of the ACTS of the Apostles in Plain English!) By The Worldwide People's Revolution!® Book 063.** Therefore, above all Things, do not Deprive yourself of those Most Enlightening Words of Provable Truths, lest you should be the Last to Enter into the Holy Kingdom of All that is GOOD! †‡

03-04 [_] O Selected King of the Ignorant Fools, if any Government began to Mint and Print an Unlimited Supply of New Money — such as American 100-dollar Bills — it would soon Cause

Great INFLATION, whereby it would soon Cost a Billion Dollars for just one Loaf of Stale Devitalized White Bread! Yes, you must Remember the Great Depression of the 1930's, when Germans had to pack a whole Wheelbarrow full of Money, just to Buy a single Loaf of Bread! Therefore, that Evil Plan has been Experimented with, and found Guilty as Charged with INFLATION, which is only slightly Worse than Deflation, whereby the Manufacturer or Farmer cannot get enough Money for his Product to Cover the Costs of Producing that Product, whereby he goes Broke — Thanks to the GAMBLING Money Games of those EDOMITES, who have Established a Great FALSE Economy, which is Based on the Production and Sales of Capitalist TRASH, which everyone could Live Happily without: beCause it is Possible and most Practical to Produce Good Quality Products that are Needed — such as those **"GLORIOUS Swanky Hotels Castles and Fortresses!" (Beautiful Planned City States for WISE Intelligent Well-Educated People with Common Sense and Good Understanding!) By The Worldwide People's Revolution!®**, Book 019, which Practice **"The LUSCIOUS All-Mineral Organic Method of Gardening!" (HOW to Grow DELICIOUS Satisfying Foods for Potential Kingz and Kweenz in Beautiful Swanky PALACES!)**, Book 021, which is a Companion Book of: **"Orgimmick Gardening at its Best!" (HOW to Grow Delicious Satisfying Foods without a 10-Million-Dollar Investment!)**, Book 079, which contains many Enlightening Photographs with Explanations that will Blow Out all of that INFLATION and DEFLATION, and Send it to Hell, where it Belongs with Satan and Sons, Incorporated, who is in Charge of the Financial Synagogue of Satan on Wall Street, which Controls Main Street! †§‡§§

03-05 [_] Well, my Potential Enemy, you Completely Failed to HEAR what I Said; and therefore, you Misinterpreted it unto your own Great Shame: beCause I did not Say to Print any Phony American Paper Money, much less to Give it to any Fake News Broadcasters; but, I Said to Establish a New RIGHTEOUS One-World GovernMINT, which will Mint and Print the Necessary New Money — NOT to Give it Away, nor to Loan it to anyone; but, to use it WISELY, in Order to HIRE whomever is Willing and Able to Learn and WORK: beCause all such Money must be EARNED by Honest Labor, without any Loans, and without any Taxes: beCause Taxes are only Collected by WICKED ANTI-CHRIST FALSE Governments! Indeed, just Imagine how many Taxes would be Needed, if everyone in the Whole World should Learn, Believe, Love, and OBEY **"The New MAGNIFIED Version of the 20 Commandments!"** †

03-06 [_] O Unselected King, I have never even Heard of the 20 Commandments. Therefore, you must be INSANE!

03-07 [_] You have Failed to Study: **"LIGHTNING STRIKES Versus Lightning Bugs!" (HOW you can Become Moderately RICH, without Telling any Lies nor Selling any Trash!) By The Worldwide People's Revolution!®**, Book 074, which contains **"The New MAGNIFIED Version of the 20 Commandments!"** — along with other Enlightening Information — such as: **"WHO QUALIFIES to Rule Over US?"** Trust me, there will be ZERO Inflation on that New Money: beCause it will have to be EARNED by Honest Labor, just to Build those **"GLORIOUS Swanky Hotels Castles and Fortresses!"** — all of which will Represent that New Money, which will make it the very Best Money in all of the World: beCause it will have something of True Value to Represent it, being much Better than the Finest of Pure Gold, Silver, Rubies and Diamonds! Indeed, you should now Ask yourself, "What Represents our Present Money?" — followed by, "What is the Actual Value of Diamonds, seeing that there are HUGE Warehouses full of TRILLIONS of them?" ‡ (See *Wikipedia* for the Proof.)

(HOW to be Liberated from all Slavery, Worldwide!)

03-08 [_] O Elected King of all Intelligent People, Worldwide, I will now tell you what Represents our Phony Money — it is the TRASH in the Trash Dump, the Old Junked Cars in the Junkyards, and the almost Worthless Wooden / Plastic Firetrap Mouse-infested Cockroach Dens, which Americans call their "Dream Homes," which can Burn Up within 20 Minutes, or Blow Away within 2 or 3 Seconds! Yes, if they do not Blow Away, nor Burn Up, the Termites Eat them, or else they just ROT DOWN: beCause they are Extremely TRASHY Houses, which Require Constant Repairs, Painting, and Insurance, which never Covers the Cost of Insurance, itself: beCause it is another Edomite Scam! Therefore, I am going to Join **The Worldwide People's Revolution!®**, and Help you to Publish this Inspired Book, with the Hope that we can put those Edomites OUT of Business: beCause they have Robbed us Long Enough. †§‡

03-09 [_] Well, my Friend, you have made a very Wise Decision: beCause, once the Words of Truths get Publish, Worldwide, the Babylonian Empire will FALL, and none of those Worthless Houses will be found for Sale: beCause no one will Want any of them, once they Discover that they can be Eating at **Royal Swanky Buffets** within those **"GLORIOUS Swanky Hotels Castles and Fortresses,"** which are Designed for True Prosperity, which have large Spacious All-Mineral Organic Gardens, Vineyards and Orchards, whereby no one can go Hungry again: beCause of having a 7-year Supply of Foods in their Walk-in Coolers, Root Cellars, Freezers, and Pantries — Thanks to **"The Swanky Associations of Working Soldiers!" (A Fascinating Collection of Various Kinds of Voluntary Working Soldiers!) By The Worldwide People's Revolution!®** Book 018. Yes, they will Join **"Seven Great Armies of Working Soldiers!" (HOW to Provide a Way for Everyone to WORK: so as to Eliminate Poverty, Crimes, Drug Abuses, Prisons and Unnecessary Taxes!) By The Worldwide People's Revolution!®** Book 015. Therefore, **"Are you a Jobless Graduate of the SKQL uv FQLZ?"** See Google for: **"HOW to Get a GOUD EJUKAASHUN without Robbing the Bank!"** Book 020.

03-10 [_] O Elected King, I already have a Good Education; but, I must Confess that I am a Jobless Graduate of the Public School of Ignorant Fools. {See www.Amazon.com for: **"The Public School of IGNERUNT FQLZ!" (HOW we have been GRAATLEE DISEEVD by Capitalism!)** Book 024, which is a Companion Book of: **"In thu Beeginingz uv Thingz!" (Thu Kreeaashun Stooree frum thu Beegining!) By The Worldwide People's Revolution!®** Book 025.}

— Chapter 04 —

Why do the Edomites Think of us Tax Slaves as Beasts?

04-01 [_] Like it or not, when certain Weak-minded People — aka George Warmonger Bush, Little Dick Chicanery, and Donald Trumpeter, Incorporated — become Excessively Rich with the False Riches, they just Naturally Think of themselves as being Superior to other People, as if they were the Hottest Bull Dung in the Barnyard, which is really not their Faults: beCause they did not Design the Human Body, nor their own Minds. Therefore, they cannot Rightly be Blamed for their Inherited Mental Disease, which we could Blame onto those Biblical Authors, who Failed to WARN us about the Dangers of Edomite Traps, you might say — such as Borrowing Money for Building or Buying an almost Worthless House, rather than Save our Money for Building a Beautiful Swanky Stone Dome Home Complex, which would Require at least a thousand Years of Savings by some Poor Hardworking Person: beCause of the Small Amount of Fake Fiat Money that one might Earn in such a False Economy. †§‡

04-02 [_] O Selected King of **The Worldwide People's Revolution!®**, are you Sure that God did not Want all such People to be Tested by the Temptations and Pitfalls of Capitalism? Indeed, it is somewhat Like the Forbidden Fruit in the Garden of Eden, which Adam and Eve could have Ignored, if they had Set their Minds on it; but, by Means of that Lying Snake, Eve was Deceived, who Yielded to the Great Temptation of Eating the Forbidden Fruit, whereby she Vainly Imagined that she would become Wise, like God, even as many Modern Women have Yielded to the Temptations of False Riches, and have been Pursuing the Invisible Angel of False Prosperity, who is always Miles Ahead of them, Luring them on toward a Hellish Condition, which he calls the "American Dream," which is Actually an American Nightmare! Yes, it is otherwise known as SLAVERY; but, it is Painted as "True Freedom" on Big Banners, which are Forever Waved High throughout the Cursed Land of Education Slaves, Work Slaves, Tax Slaves, Insurance Slaves, Interest Slaves, College Loan Debt Slaves, Mortgage Slaves, Rent Slaves, Credit Card Debt Slaves, Endless Bills Slaves, and all of those other Kinds of Slaves that you Forgot about, including the Sex Slaves, who are more Numerous now than during the so-called "Dark Ages," being the Victims of Satan's most Deceptive Economic System, called CAPITALISM, which Appears to make X-amount of People RICH, while making all of the People into Slaves of one Kind or another, who have Great Faith in that False Economic System: beCause X-amount of Witty People have "Succeeded" with making themselves more Wealthy than the others, who were Actually Born to be the Masters of this World, who have simply taken Advantage of their Weak-minded Servants, who would have no Idea what to Do without some Masters of some Kind to Manage them. Indeed, it is not Commonly Known that nearly half of the Freed Negro Slaves during the 1860's Willingly Chose to Remain with their Masters: beCause they were the more Intelligent ones among them, who could Foresee what was Coming by the Grand Deceptions of the Edomites, who Arranged for them to Inherit 40 Acres of Land and a Mule — as if a Person could Earn a Living on such a Small Piece of Unproductive Land with only one Mule, which did not even Multiply itself. Therefore, almost all of them were Forced to Borrow Money, just to Build a Shanty; and then they were Forced by their Circumstances to make themselves into Work Slaves for New "Democratic" Masters, just to Repay their Loans; and thus they got themselves into Worse Conditions than they were when they were Slaves on the Plantations, when they at least had Good Foods to Eat from their Gardens, Vineyards and Orchards. In Fact, Multitudes of them Departed from their Lands, and Moved into Hateful Cities of Confusion, and made themselves into Capitalist Prostitutes of Various Kinds, just to Survive: beCause they did not know what else to Do! Indeed, there were no Preachers Loudly Proclaiming the Good News that you Teach, O Selected King: beCause no such Inspired Words of Provable Truths can be Discovered within that so-called "Holy Bible," which does not even Reveal what a Righteous Government would Do for Obtaining any Money, much less Trillions of Dollars, except to TAX the Work Slaves for it, whose Minds cannot be Enlightened by any Means: beCause they are Blinded by their PRIDE, even as a Soldier is Taught to be very Proud, when he should be most Humble and Honest: beCause he is in Danger of Dying at just any Time, and long before Living a Good Life. Yes, he is Identified as a "Serviceman," which Means that he is Expected to SERVE his Country, and for Minimum Wages in most Cases. †§‡

04-03 [_] For Example, **"The Divided States of United Lies"** paid its Murderous Soldiers about 48 Dollars per Month during World War 2, which most of them Sent Home to Help Feed their Parents, Younger Brothers and Sisters: because the Military provided those Sailors and Soldiers with Rations of Food, Clothing, and Muddy Trenches to Live in and Sleep on Hard Ground, or Sleep on Tiny Cots in Crowded Ships in Angry Seas, which never Ceased to Toss and Roll them all about. Personally, I would much Prefer by a thousand Times to be the Humble Servant of a Rich One-World Government, which Provides all that I Need for Living a Good Life and Working at HOME, within one of those **"Beautiful Swanky PALACES!" (A New Concept in Living Habits — Swanky Palaces for Poor People!) By The Worldwide People's Revolution!®** Book 066. Yes, I Know, it would Require a LOT of Hard Work to get those Palaces Built, even with the Assistance of Mechanical Slaves; but, once they are Finished, we can all Relax for the next 10,000 or more Years, and Count our Blessings, one by one — such as the Great Blessing of not having any more Hateful Wars, Worldwide: beCause all of the People who Join those **"Seven Great Armies of Working Soldiers"** will eventually get to Live in Peace, with True Prosperity, and will thus Forget about Wars: beCause they will all be Secure within their Swanky Fortresses. ‡

04-04 [_] Well, my Friend, it Sounds like a Wonderful Utopian Dream that is about to come True for those Wise People who BELIEVE: beCause it only Requires just ONE such Glorious Swanky Fortress to Persuade all of the other Wise People in the Whole World to Join Forces with them: beCause of having Quick Means of Communicating with all Peoples. Indeed, just Visualize how a Normal Work Slave would Feel to get an E-mail Letter from a Trusted Friend, who says something like this: I only have to Work for 4 Hours per Day, 6 Days per Week, or the Equivalent thereof — such as 8 Hours per Day this Week, and next Week Off; or, I can Work for a Month, and have a Whole Month Off — in Exchange for Living in a Beautiful Swanky Palace, which has a **Royal Swanky Buffet**, which Serves no less than a thousand Delicious Dishes of Organically-grown Foods, for FREE: beCause everything is Organized Properly by **"The Swanky Associations of Working Soldiers!" (A Fascinating Collection of Various Kinds of Voluntary Working Soldiers!) By The Worldwide People's Revolution!®** Book 018. For Example, just one Well-Built Strong Young Man can Dig Up enough Potatoes by Hand within 4 Hours to Feed 200 People: beCause the Topsoil is 3 feet deep, being Prepared Properly by **"The LUSCIOUS All-Mineral Organic Method of Gardening!" (HOW to Grow DELICIOUS Satisfying Foods for Potential Kingz and Kweenz in Beautiful Swanky PALACES!) By The**

Worldwide People's Revolution!® Book 021. Therefore, why should he have to Work for 8 Hours or more every Day, just to Live? Indeed, I have no Intentions of BUYING any Part of any Swanky Palace: beCause I am not Deceived by that Ownership Nonsense, which is just another Edomite LIE: beCause the President Lives in a Palace, which he does not Own. Likewise, the Pope of Rome Lives in a Palace that he did not Buy, and I am Sure that he is just as Happy for it as if he Owned it: beCause it is all in a Person's Mind. Therefore, just Forget about any Private Property, even as the Disciples of Jesus Christ Forgot about it, and Sold all that they had, and Laid Down their Moneys at the Feets of the Apostles, who Distributed the Money to everyone who had any Need for it, whereby they all became Moderately RICH: beCause they Shared their Lands, Houses, Tools, and Work with each other, who Forgot to go into the Fine Details to Explain it all to us. However, you can Discover the Whole Truth of it in a Wonderful Book, called: **"The New MAGNIFIED Version of the Book of ACTS!" (The Understandable Version of the ACTS of the Apostles in Plain English!) By The Worldwide People's Revolution!**® Book 063. ‡

04-05 [_] O Elected King of the Highest Mountains of Godly Wisdom, I would Think that you could Round Up no less than a Million Americans, who would be Happy to Help you to Build one of those Trillion-dollar Swanky Fortresses, and with Voluntary Labor, if there were some Way to Guarantee each Family to have a Swanky Stone Dome Home Complex to Live in; but, I Seriously Doubt that the Federal Government would go along with any such Plan: beCause they just Naturally Want to Collect their TAXES, whereby they would Tax the Property right out from under all of you, and leave you with nothing, just like they already did to you and your Brother Vern, which we can read all about in: **"LIGHTNING STRIKES Versus Lightning Bugs!" (HOW you can Become Moderately RICH, without Telling any Lies nor Selling any Trash!) By The Worldwide People's Revolution!**® Book 074.

04-06 [_] O Elected King, there must be some other more Humble Nation of Wiser People, who would Love your Master Plan, who would Help you to Build at least one Beautiful Swanky Palace for a Demonstration to the Whole World. Indeed, I Suggest that the Israelis might do it for the Poor Palestinians, whereby they could make Friends with them, and Stop Persecuting them by Stealing their Lands. ‡

04-07 [_] Well, that Sounds like a Great Idea, whose Time has now Come; but, what are the Chances of those Edomites Allowing it to Happen, seeing that they would have to Sacrifice their Pride on the Altar of Love? 🔔

04-08 [_] O Elected King, those Poor Israelis do not have a Trillion Dollars to Spend on the Building Materials, even if they Wanted to Build any of those **"Beautiful Swanky PALACES!" (A New Concept in Living Habits — Swanky Palaces for Poor People!) By The Worldwide People's Revolution!**® Book 066. Therefore, they would be Forced by their Extreme Poverty to DEMAND: **"The Great Worldwide TELEVISED Court HEARING!" (That Great Meeting of the Most Intelligent and Well-Educated Minds!) By The Worldwide People's Revolution!**®, Book 041, whereby they might Establish **"The New RIGHTEOUS One-World Government!" (HOW to Establish a Righteous One-World Government without Going to WAR!) By The Worldwide People's Revolution!**®, Book 056, whereby they might Obtain an Unlimited Supply of Good Money for Doing Good Works, and without any Property Taxes, nor even any Income Taxes: beCause everyone would just Cheerfully Donate whatever TITHE

Money might be Needed for Operating such a Good Government, even as the Israelites of Old Donated their Tithe Money to Moses and Joshua, who used it Wisely to Build the First Swanky Fortress in Saudi Arabia, which is still Standing Firm after thousands of Years, right next to Mount Sinai, being Occupied by Skunks, Snakes, Bats and Screech Owls: beCause there is not one Person in a thousand, or perhaps one in a million, who would Want to Live in a CAVE HOUSE, under the Terraced Gardens, as you Propose: beCause all such Places are DAMP and Cold with their Stone Domes. Indeed, they do not Stop to Think about it, and Consider the Fact that it is Possible to Build ICE Houses under those Stone Dome Homes, which SUCK OUT the Moisture from the Houses, while also Providing Ice for Coolers, Freezers, and Root Cellars: beCause the Temperatures in all such Worthless Deserts drop down to Freezing, almost every Night, which can make Ice Water in large Ice Trays, which is then easily Frozen by Means of ElecTrickery, which is Produced by WIND Power all around the Fortress, which is Captured in Stone Arcades of Funnels at the Tops of all of the Tall Stone Walls, even as the following Drawings show. †§‡§§

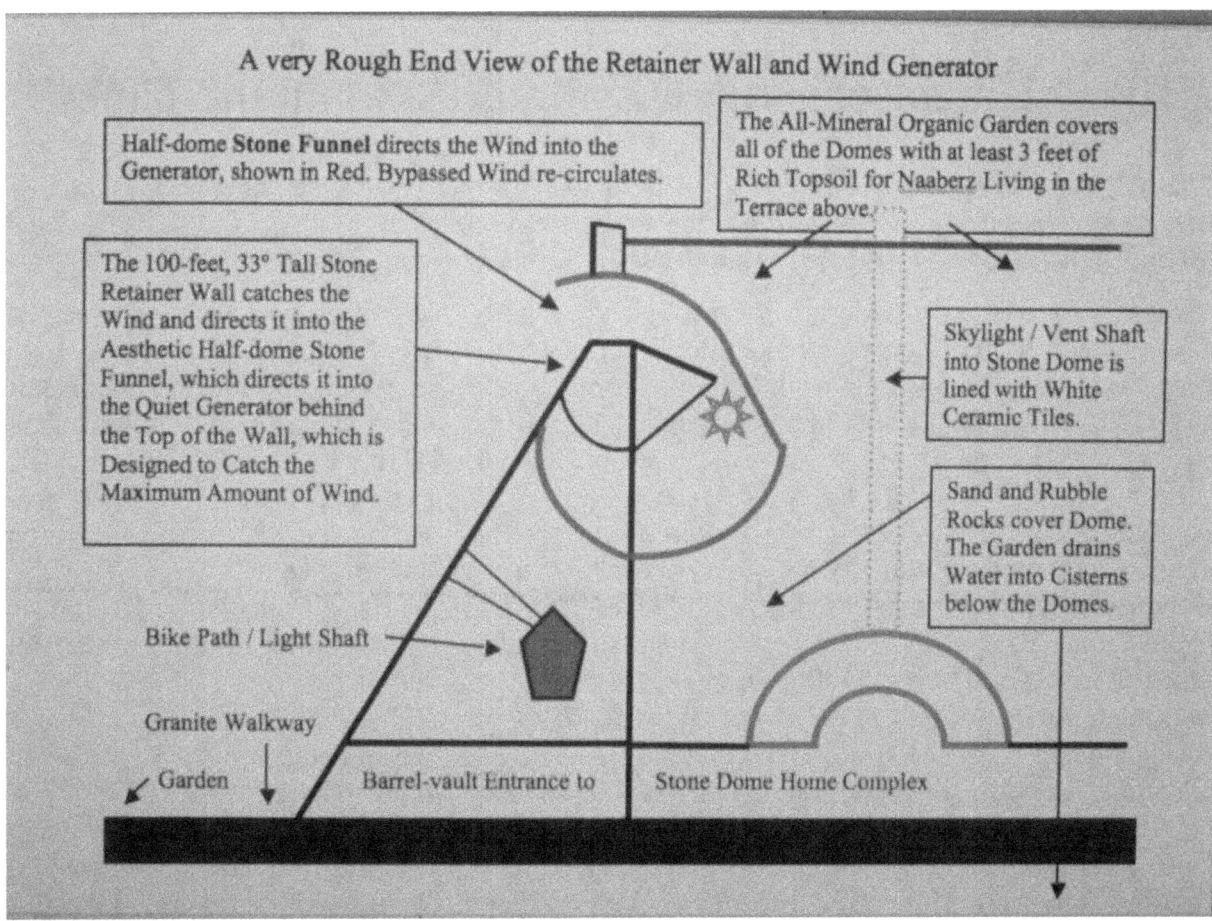

04-09 [_] Well, my Sarcastic Friend, it is another one of my Great Ideas, whose Time has now come for Providing FREE ElecTrickery for all Wise People: beCause the Wind never Stops Blowing at the Tops of all such Tall Stone Walls, at least from one Direction or another, which anyone can Discover by taking a Walk to the Top of the Great Pyramid of the Sun, near Mexico City. Therefore, having Tall Stone Walls for at least 4 Terraces around all Swanky Fortresses, will make it Possible to Capture the Wind for Producing Free Electric Power from then on, which can be used Wisely for Pumping Water from Lower Cisterns to Higher Cisterns for "Battery Backup Power," while also Producing Pure Living Water in thousands of Waterfalls. §‡

04-10 [_] O Elected King of **"The New RIGHTEOUS One-World Government,"** I can hardly Wait to See those **"GLORIOUS Swanky Hotels Castles and Fortresses"** Finished! Indeed, we will Need about 2 Million of them, just to Accommodate the 7+ Billion People in this World of Wonders, which will Require about 30 Years to Finish all of them, if we go to Work on them like going to War, using Mechanical Slaves to do 90% or more of the Heavy Work. However, in the Meantime, I would like to Read the Original Book, which was Suppressed by Amazon, called: **"Are we Tax Slaves of a Lower Order than Lying Red Jews?" (HOW to be Liberated from all Slavery, Worldwide!) By The Leader — Adolf Dictator Hitler, Junior!** ‡

— Chapter 05 —

The Original Book, Slightly Modified to Fit the Times!

{HEADNOTE: Please Check any Boxes with Statements that you Agree with. Thank you. The first Chapter is taken from the Introduction to the Book, followed by the entire Book; and the Introduction was by "Adolf Hitler," himself, whom I Impersonated with Literary License.}

05-01 [_] God Forbid that I should Speak in any Public Place, being an Outcast of Society, having a very BAD Reputation among the Masses of so-called "Educated" People, who have been Thoroughly Brainwashed with Edomite Propagandist LIES, which my Adopted Son, Adolf Hitler, Junior, has pointed out in this Inspired Book for your Enlightenment and True Education with a Capital E. Therefore, this Unique Book is COPYRIGHTED 2016—20016 AD, by The Leader — Adolf Dictator Hitler, Junior! Indeed, all Rights are Reserved for the Truth's Sake. No Portion of this Good Book shall be Reproduced by any Means for Sale without Written Permission from the Author {who is now known as **The Worldwide People's Revolution!®**}. However, with his Permission, anyone and everyone in the World is Welcome to Reproduce Exact Copies of this Book, and Sell them for a Reasonable Profit, and KEEP 90% of the Net Profits for their own Peace and Prosperity: because the Author only wants 10% of the Net Profits for the Construction of **"The Great World TEMPLE of PEACE,"** which will be the Headquarters for **"The New RIGHTEOUS One-World Government,"** which will have an Unlimited Supply of New Money, with his own Face on the Money, which that Good Government will use Wisely to HIRE whomever is Willing and Able to Learn and Work, in Order to Help Build those **"GLORIOUS Swanky Hotels Castles and Fortresses!" (Beautiful Planned City States for WISE Intelligent Well-Educated People with Common Sense and Good Understanding!)**, Book 019, which will Solve more than 5,000 Major and Minor Problems in this World of Woes, including the Unemployment Problem, the Low-Wages Problem, the Tax Slavery Problem, the Insurance Slavery Problem, the Drug Slavery Problem, the Interest / Usury Slavery Problem, the Sex Trafficking Problem, the Illegal Immigration Problem, the Illegal Drug Trafficking Problem, the Terrorist Attacks, Poverty, Hunger, Riots, Strikes, Water Shortages, Climate Changing Problems, and so on and so on — even an "Endless" Array of PROBLEMS! †§‡

(HOW to be Liberated from all Slavery, Worldwide!)

05-02 [_] In other words, those Lying Edomites are going to Learn HOW to Cooperate with the Honest White Israelites, who are Symbolized by People like Jesus Christ and his Beloved Disciples, or else those Lying Edomites will be put Out of Business. Therefore, this Inspired Book is Copyrighted AD 2016, by the so-called "Dictator," Adolf Hitler, Junior, whose Selected King has full Intentions of taking over this Insane World by whatever Means is Necessary: because it Desperately Needs someone in Charge of it, which every Honest Person on this Earth Agrees with. However, if you Disagree, please Check with an X the Appropriate Boxes below, which have Statements that you Agree with. {See: **"Our Elected King Who Speaks Out!" (It is High Time for some Sane Person to Get Control of this Insane World!) By The Worldwide People's Revolution!® Book 080.**}

A-[_] I Agree — this World Desperately Needs some Honest Human Being in Charge of it: beCause, as of now, it is Obvious that it is Managed by SATAN, the Devil, whose Chief Servants are those Lying EDOMITES! ‡

B-[_] I Believe that Adolf Hitler would have been a Good Leader, if he had been put in Charge of this World in 1930, whereby Americans, Brits, Europeans, Asians, and Africans would not have Suffered through the Great Edomite Depression of the 1930's. For Example, when Adolf Hitler became the Dictator of Germany in 1933, 30% of Germans were Unemployed, and Edomite Inflation was so Bad that it Required a Wheelbarrow full of Money to Buy just one Loaf of Bread; but, 6 Months later, with a True Leader in Command, there was Zero Unemployment, and one could Buy a Loaf of Bread for only 4 Deutschmarks. Therefore, it is Extremely Easy to Understand WHY the German People LOVED Adolf Hitler, who Rode in Parades within Open Cars, up until 1939. Moreover, within 6 Years of his Leadership, it Required the Combined Forces of the entire Capitalist and Communist Worlds to Defeat those Rich Germans. Facts First. ‡

C-[_] I Confess that I am Extremely Ignorant about that Part of World History. Indeed, I am far too Young to have Experienced it, nor do I even Care about it: beCause I Live for TODAY and Tomorrow: beCause I am an Optimistic Capitalist, not a Murderous Communist, nor a Socialist with Unsociable Insecurity Checks for Survival. §

D-[_] DUMBmocracy would have never put Adolf Hitler on Election Ballots: beCause it would have been BAD for the Great False Economy, which Depends on Deceptions and Edomite Lies — such as People going to Heaven when they Die, which gives to them a Great False HOPE that their Future in Heaven will Render Justice for ALL, including Justice for the Billions of Victims of Edomite Propagandist Lies, whereby they were made into Rebellious and Humiliated Education Slaves, Work Slaves, Tax Slaves, Interest Slaves, Insurance Slaves, Drug Slaves, Sex Slaves, Childcare Slaves, Gas Slaves, Rent Slaves, Transportation Slaves, and Endless Bills Slaves. {See www.Amazon.com for: **"The Great False Economy is now DEBUNKED!" (Adolf Hitler had a Much Better Economic System!) By The Worldwide People's Revolution!® Book 053.**}

E-[_] Educated People know that Election Deceptions are RIGGED in Favor of 2 Main Political Parties — at least in **"The Divided States of United Lies!" (The so-called "United States of North America" in Disguise!)**, Book 058, whereby Competing Political Parties are "laid to rest" by the Evil System of Election Deceptions, whose

Political Candidates seldom mention the Important Issues of the Time, much less Present any Reasonable Solutions for our Massive Problems. For Example, what are their **"Guaranteed Solutions"** for no more Car Accidents, no more Teenage Suicides, no more Gang Wars, no more School Shootings, no more Mass Murders, no more Illegal Immigrations, and no more Illegal Drugs? †§‡ {See: **"Guaranteed Solutions!" (HOW to Solve our Local and Global Problems in the Most Rational Manner Possible!) By The Worldwide People's Revolution!®** Book 080.}

F-[_] I Fail to Understand what this Insane Book is all about. Why are so many Words Capitalized?

G-[_] God knows that you need to keep on Reading with a Capital R. {See the above Link on the Internet for: **"Justifications for Capitalizations!" (WHY our Elected King Defies the School of Fools by Capitalizing LOVE and HATE!)**, Book 049.}

H-[_] Humble and Honest People only need to Read the *Holy Bible,* and NOT with a Capital R: beCause it does not matter whether or not one Actually Believes anything that is written in the *Holy Bible,* just so long as he or she Believes in Jesus Christ enough to Love and OBEY him, who is the One and ONLY Savior of the World — NOT Adolf Hitler, Junior, nor any other Fascist Fraud, Dictator, nor Elected King! †§‡§§ {See: **"Are Americans the Most STUPID People who ever Lived?" (HOW Working People can PROSPER and Live in PEACE Under the Rulership of a RIGHTEOUS KING!) By The Worldwide People's Revolution!®** Book 047.}

I-[_] I Object to your Insults against the Words of God, who said, *"Mankind shall not Live by Physical Foods, alone; but, also by every Word that proceeds from the Mouths of the Gods, who are the Supreme Rulers of Heavens and Earths without Number, whose Governors are Identified as KINGS, who have Power and Authority over their King Domes, whose Voluntary Servants Cheerfully Obey them: beCause they Understand that it is for their own Good."* — New MAGNIFIED Version (NMV) of *Matthew 4:4.* †§‡

J-[_] I Judge that you have Added Lies to the Words of God: beCause there is only ONE God, who is Jesus Christ, himself, who Prayed to himself in the Garden of Gethsemane, saying: *"Father, if you are Willing, please Remove this Cup of Bitterness from me; nevertheless, not my Will be Done; but, your Will be Done on the Earth, even as it is now Done in Heavenly Places."* — NMV of *Luke 22:42.* †§‡

K-[_] King Jesus will have your Lying Tongue CUT OUT: beCause *that* is NOT Exactly what that *Scripture* states in the Gay King James Version. †§‡

L-[_] Lots of Laughs! Nobody would Know for Sure what any *Scriptures* state: beCause there are more than 200 Translations of them, and all of them are wRong, or else there would not be so many Translations. Indeed, that might also Explain WHY we have a Right-WRong Political Party, and a Rong-Riit Party to Vote for, who Identify themselves as Dimwitcrats and Reprobates, who would never take up their Swords of Truths in an Intellectual Battle with our Selected King: because they Know for a Fact that they would be Defeated by him! But, if not, why do they not Invite him to Speak at a 3-hour Joint Session of both Houses of Congress, including the President and the Low Court of Supreme Injustices, who Claim to be Superior to him, just beCause of having Degrees from Universities, while our Selected King is a Grade School DROPOUT, being a Near Relative of Jesus Christ, himself!? †§‡§§ {See: **"Our Elected King Who Speaks Out,"** Book 070, for just such a Speech, which was Delivered to both Houses of Congress, the President, Vice President, and the Supreme Court Justices, in a TOP SECRET Joint Session: beCause it could not be Published by the C-SPAN Network: beCause of the FEAR of Exposing the Lies and Deceptions of the Edomites to the General Public, who Control all such Timid Political Rabbits by Controlling the Money Supply. However, it will be Presented to all of the Nations of Wise People when we Hold **"The Great Worldwide TELEVISED Court HEARING!" (That Great Meeting of the Most Intelligent and Well-Educated Minds!) By The Worldwide People's Revolution!®** Book 041. Therefore, Exciting Times are Coming! Therefore, Sharpen up your own Sword of Provable Truths, and get yourself Prepared to Speak the Whole Truth.} †§‡

M-[ ] Neither Political Party has enough Money to Buy my Vote by Spreading Edomite Lies — such as, "We are the Freest People on the Earth," when we are nothing but Education Slaves, Work Slaves, Tax Slaves, Interest Slaves, Insurance Slaves, Drug Slaves, Credit Card Debt Slaves, Rent Slaves, Mortgage Slaves, Transportation Slaves, ElecTricky Bills Slaves, Gas Bills Slaves, Water Bills Slaves, and Endless Bills Slaves. Indeed, we are anything except a Free People with a Capital F, whereby we might be Free like a Wild Mountain Goat, who has NO Bills, NO Debts, NO Taxes, NO Insurance, NO Drugs, and NO Aches nor Pains, much less Divorces, a Broken Heart, and a Wounded Soul: beCause of some Selfish Greedy Capitalist BITCH, who is not Contented to Imitate Mother Mary, who was Dedicated to Raising Up an Innocent Child called Jesus Christ! No wonder 90% of the Women in the World, who are Killed by Guns, are Killed in **"The Divided States of United Lies!"** †§‡ (Ask Representative Chellie Pingree, a Democrat from Maine, if you Doubt it. See *General Speeches* on C-SPAN for June 21st, 2016.)

N-[ ] Not everyone is Interested in Government Affairs, much less in Electing some Lying Deceiving Politicians, who are Puppets on the Strings of Lying Edomite Bankers, who Control the Money Supply, who Determine the Fates of all Nations. For Example, they brought about the Great Depression of the 1930's, just by Withholding their Money from the People, who Desperately Needed it, including Farmers, who Suffered with Droughts, who had no Huge Cisterns for Water Storage, as they should have. Yes, the Cry went out that Banks were BROKE, and had no Money to Loan, which was True of Little Banks; but, NOT of Giant Goliath Banks. In Fact, tens of thousands of little Bankers went Out of Business, Worldwide; but, NOT the Big Edomite Banksters, who Gained hundreds of Billions of Dollars by Means of what they called "Foreclosures" on American Houses, Vehicles and Furniture, which their Interest / Usury Slaves had not yet Paid for. Moreover, they began Collecting Trillions of Dollars just as soon as we got into World War 2: beCause, within just one or 2 Weeks, after the United States Declared War on Japan and Germany, those same Greedy Bankers suddenly came up with hundreds of Billions of Dollars for Loaning it to the Federal Government of **"The Divided States of United Lies,"** which used it Wisely for Building Millions of Airplanes, Army Tanks, Trucks, Jeeps, Boats, Ships, Aircraft Carriers, Submarines, Radars, Uniforms, Rifles,

Bullets, Bombs, Mortars, Big Guns, Grenades, Bazookas, Mess Kits, Gas Masks, Tents, Cots, Sleeping Bags, Sweaty Insulated Boots, thousands of Propagandist Movies, Advertisements for Volunteer Soldiers, and everything that was Necessary for going to WAR: beCause those Wars are Extremely Profitable for Rich Edomites, who Own most of the Military Industrial Congressional Bankers' News-Media Hollywood-Movie Book-Publishing Chemical-Corporation Drug-Industry COMPLEX, if ye Knows what I Means, O Nigger Jim? But, if thou doth not Knoweth what I Meaneth, thou shouldst Ask Tom Sawyer or Huck Finn, after they have been Enlightened. †§‡§§ {See *The Adventures of Tom Sawyer and Huck Finn with Nigger Jim* by Mark Twain, who would now have a much Better Book to Publish, called: **"Are we Tax Slaves of a Lower Order than those Lying EDOMITES!" (HOW to be Liberated from all Slavery, Worldwide!) By The Worldwide People's Revolution!®**, Book 052, which is this Book. See: **"The UGLY Scarred Dishonest Face of Poor Old Miserable UNCLE SAM!" (A Memorial Day Legacy!) By The Worldwide People's Revolution!®**, Book 054, which is a Companion Book of: **"The United States of the Whole World!" (A True Global Economy for the Masses of Working People!) By The Worldwide People's Revolution!®** Book 055.}

O-[_] Are there no OPTIONS to Choose from? Why do we not Build Beautiful Planned City States, called: **"GLORIOUS Swanky Hotels Castles and Fortresses!" (Beautiful Planned City States for WISE Intelligent Well-Educated People with Common Sense and Good Understanding!) By The Worldwide People's Revolution!®**, Book 019, which are made up of Like-minded People, who get to Choose the Kind of Governments that they Want, *as Opposed to having at least half of the People Continually Unhappy?* For Example, some People like to Abort their Babies, while others call it Murder. Therefore, they can Separate themselves from one another, and thus Live in Peace. Likewise, half of the People are against Private Citizens having Weapons, while the other half would like to Live in the Wild West Days, when almost all of the Men Packed their Firearms for Self-defense. Therefore, let them Live with People of Like-mindedness. Moreover, not even half of Americans bothered themselves to Vote during the last General Election Deception: beCause they Knew that nothing would Change, in spite of many Promises to Change the System, and to make this a Better World. Therefore, the Political Parade to Hell goes on and on: beCause almost all of the Politicians are Working for the Military Industrial Congressional Bankers' Complex, which has been Deliberately made so Complicated that the Normal Person cannot even Understand it. Yes, it is as Mysterious as the Evil Events of September 11th, 2001, which Produced at least a thousand Unanswered Questions. For Example, what Happened to the Blood and Guts of the People who supposedly Crashed into a Field near Shanksville, Pennsylvania? †§‡§§ (See the many YouTube Videos for the Irrefutable Evidences.)

P-[_] Politicians do not like to Talk about any such Gory Subjects: beCause the Federal Burden of Investigation (FBI) and the Central Unintelligent Agencies (CIA) already made a Thorough Investigation into all of those Evil Events, and came up with a 500+page book, called *THE 9/11 COMMISSION REPORT,* which did not even Mention the Destruction of World Trade Center Tower 7, which came Crashing Down at 5:20 P.M., during September 11th, 2001, in the form of DUST, whereby there were only a few Truckloads of Debris left in a Small Pile, even after 283 Hardened Steel Columns (many of which were 22-inches by 52-inches by 47-stories tall) collapsed in Unison, like Ballet Dancers hitting the Floor, in less than 7 Seconds, and without making a Hole in the so-called "Concrete Bathtub," which prevented the Hudson River from Flooding the entire Area with Water! Yes, many Americans are Amazed by those Facts, which are Revealed by www.AE911TRUTH.org for your Enlightenment, if you have the Spiritual Fortitude to Investigate it for yourself. (See: *Experts Speak Out,* and go about Proving them to be WRong, if you can. Remember that more than 3,000 Architects and Engineers Agree with them and Dr. Judy Wood, who Noticed very Strange Things in New Yuck City!) Most Shameless Persnickety Americans do not Agree, who Dismiss the entire Evil Event by saying something like this: "Those are all Things of the Past. I Believe in the Admonition of the Apostle Paul, who said that we should *'Forget those Evil Things that are Behind us, and Press Forward to those Good Things that are in Front of us.'* — *Philippians 3:13, NMV.* And that would NOT Mean to be Looking Forward to the Building of Beautiful Planned City States: because, *'We Look for a Holy City, whose Foundations are made of Colorful Stones, which are 1,500 Miles High, which Holy City is made without Human Hands, whose Builder and Maker is GOD and his Holy Angels!'* even as it is written in *Hebrews 11:10 and Revelation 21.*" †§‡§§ {See: **"Those Ridiculous Contradictions within the Holy Bible!" (HOW to Read the Mutilated Bible with an Open Mind!) By The Worldwide People's Revolution!® Book 057.**}

Q-[_] The Great Question is this: **"How much MONEY did those Lying Edomites GAIN by Orchestrating the Evil Events of September 11th, 2001?"** And the Answer is: TRILLIONS of Dollars! Yes, it all made it Possible for George Warmonger Bush and Little Dick Chicanery, Incorporated, to Attack IRAQ, which had no Connection with the Evil Events of September 11th, 2001; but, that Event gave George and Little Dick "Chainy" an EXCUSE for going to War: because that is HOW those Lying Edomites FILLED their Coffers with our Tax Money! Yes, it is called a "False Flag" Operation, which you can read about in *Wikipedia,* which References to several American False Flag Operations for our Education, even though it Fails to List ALL of them, which will be Exposed at: **"The Great Worldwide TELEVISED Court HEARING!"** Book 041. And thus *Wikipedia* will have to be Updated to Fit the Realities of Life and Death. †§‡

R-[_] I Refuse to Study any such Ridiculous Conspiracy Theories by Radical Racist Anti-Christ Communist Sympathizers of the Anti-Semitic Neo-Nazi Penguin Party, who have Cold Stony Hearts without any Empathy for Poor Old Aunt Polly, nor for the Poorer Widow Douglas, who only Want to Attend to their Knitting, and Watch Comedies on TV, after Attending Boring Church Services, where the Irreverent LOUDMOUTH Slothgut Windbag Hole-in-Thy-Head Presides in the Unholy Church of Little Faith on Hopeless Street and Suicide Avenue, who reads the Revised Standard Versions (RSV) of 200+ Mutilated Mistranslations, who Preaches LOUD Sermons to Drink-it and Nag-it, who have 3 Children, called Innocence, I-Believe, and Giving. Yes, he Drinks to Comfort himself after Wasting his Precious Time as a Work Slave and Tax Slave, and she Nags him for his Drinking, and both of them end up in the Low Court of Supreme Injustices, getting a Needless Divorce: beCause they could have been and should have been Living in one of those **"Beautiful Swanky PALACES!" (A New Concept in Living Habits — Swanky Palaces for Poor People!) By The Worldwide People's Revolution!® Book** 066. Indeed, they could all become Moderately RICH, and without Telling any Lies, nor

Selling any Trash: beCause that is Physically and Financially Possible and most Practical, and without Borrowing any Money from those Edomite Bankers, nor from any of their Lackeys: beCause of Practicing True Love, which comes with Good Understanding, which is not Blinded by any Pride! †§‡ {See: **"The New MAGNIFIED Version of the Book of ACTS!" (The Understandable Version of the ACTS of the Apostles in Plain English!) By The Worldwide People's Revolution!®** Book 063.}

S-[_] All Honest Students of the Self-Enlightened School of Higher Learning must Agree that *someone* needs to bring those Lying Edomites to COURT, and make them Prove that they did not Greatly Profit by the Wars in Afghanistan and Iraq, whereby Americans have Built Up the Greatest War Machine the World has ever known, which is Owned mostly by Lying Conniving Edomites, who also Own and Operate the Chief Banks, the Weapons Manufacturing, the Drug Companies, Hollywood Movie Productions, Book Publishing Companies, Hospitals, Chemist Laboratories, and the News Media in general, which can easily be Proven in a Courtroom to be True or False! Yes, they are the CHIEF Criminals in this World of Woes. Moreover, I am NOT Anti-Semitic: beCause I am an Honest White Jew, myself! Therefore, do not be Falsely Accusing me of being Anti-Semitic. †‡

T-[_] I Totally Agree with you, O Adolf — that this World of Woes most Definitely Needs *someone* with a Sound Mind in Charge of it; but, I am not Sure that Adolf Junior is the Riit Person. After all, we have not yet Studied the Complete Unedited SURVEYS of his VALUES, which Surveys can be found in: **"The Complete SURVEYS of our VALUES!" (SURVEYS of Religious Spiritual Political Governmental Sexual Social Moral Economic Business Labor Habitual and Miscellaneous VALUES!)**, Book 059, which can be found on www.Amazon.com with a Free Description and Book Preview, if anyone is Interested in Learning about their own Religious Spiritual Political Governmental Sexual Social Moral Business Economic Labor Habitual and Miscellaneous VALUES. † {See the above Link for: **"Mark Twain Races for the PRESIDENCY!" (The 2020 Presidential Candidates Desperately Need Some STRONG Undefeatable COMPETITION!) By The Worldwide People's Revolution!®**, Book 033, which contains the Complete Surveys of our Selected King's Values in the Checked Boxes [X] of the above Book 059.}

U-[_] I Understand that this World would be a much Better Place, if just ONE Righteous KING were in Charge of it, who has Power given to him by the Masses of People to make this a Good World to Live in. However, without the Assistance of Capitalism, it would never Work: because all Blessings come by Way of Edomite Capitalism, or Red Jew Communism — such as the Marxist Chinese Believe in. †§‡§§ {FOOTNOTE: Karl Marx was a Jew, according to *Wikipedia,* and he was the Father of Communism, from a Family of Rabbis, who became an Atheist. Vladimir Illlich Lenin was also an Atheist.}

V-[_] You obviously have your Values Upside Down, if you Vainly Imagine that Capitalism can Save the World from its Awful Woes, when it was Capitalism that brought us into this Hellish Condition, whereby the Oceans are "Filled with TRASH," the Rivers are Poisoned, the Air is Polluted, the Water is not Fit to Drink, and the Land has been Greatly Abused with Capitalist Chemicals and Poisons. Yes, you should Study: **"The Great False Economy is now DEBUNKED!" (Adolf Hitler had a Much Better**

Economic System!) By The Worldwide People's Revolution!® Book 053. Indeed, Capitalism belongs in the Trash Dump of Obsolete Economic Systems, along with Communism, Socialism, and Fascism — none of whose Adherents like to Address the Provable Truths in: **"Guaranteed Solutions!" (HOW to Solve our Local and Global Problems in the Most Rational Manner Possible!) By The Worldwide People's Revolution!®** Book 080. Therefore, they just Ignore those Solutions, and Hope that they go Away: beCause they are a Great Threat to their Evil Empires, which Require X-amount of SLAVES to do their Dirty Work. ‡ {See YouTube for: "The Palm Island, Dubai UAE — Megastructure Development," which will get you Linked in to the Realities of Capitalists, who use Slave Labor to Accomplish "Great Things." Remember that Dubai is Extremely HOT, and mostly a Desert, which has been made into a Tourist Trap, as well as a Place for Old Rich People to Retire, which I Predict will all be Abandoned: beCause the Ugly Houses have no Gardens to Feed themselves, and the Liberated Inhabitants of Swanky Fortresses will not be Interested in Feeding them when the Rains Stop. Therefore, if they were now Wise, they would Invest their Money in Beautiful Swanky Fortresses, which have no Heating nor Cooling Bills, which have Free Electricity, and Luscious Gardens that are much more Beautiful than Dubai "Miracle" Gardens. See the Footnote under the Photo on Page 66.}

W-[_] It will Require another World War to get this thing Straightened Out Properly, and the Righteous People must Win that War. In Fact, it will be Won by Jesus Christ, himself, who is that Righteous King, who alone is Qualified to Govern us: beCause he Passed his Tests of Faith, Hope, Trust, Love, Patience, Persistence, and OBEDIENCE. {See the above Link for: **"The Seven Basic Spiritual Building Blocks of LIFE!" (Faith Hope Trust Love Patience Persistence and Obedience!)**, Book 036.}

X-[_] X-amount of People will Agree with you, even as they have been Believing for Centuries, while Patiently Waiting for the Second Coming of Jesus Christ, while using his Name in Vain, continually, who has yet to Appear, who is like a Mythical Jewish Story, and not a Real Person — even as Adolf Dictator Hitler, Junior, is NOT a Real Person: beCause there is no such Person, and never was any such Person. †§‡

Y-[_] Almost everyone is Yearning for the Day of Rest, when the Earth shall Rest for a thousand Years in a State of Peace and Happiness, which we can make for ourselves, now that we have Demon-ocracy, which is otherwise known as "Mob Rulership," whereby the Masses of People get whatever they Vote for. For Example, 95% of Americans Voted to NOT Bail Out the Gangster Banksters, during 2009; but, the Wicked Anti-Christ False Cover-up Federal Government did Bail those Robbers out, anyway, at the Expense of us Tax Slaves. Therefore, if we Act Wisely, and Elect our Selected King to be our Righteous King, we will not have to Fear any Adolf Hitler, Junior, who might become a DICTATOR, and much Worse than his "Father," who might also Exterminate ALL of those Lying Edomites. Yes, he may Load them into a Special Train, which Drives into a Special Tunnel, which Train then Stops and the People are Gassed to Death by the thousands; and then, after they are all Dead, the Train Delivers their Bodies to large Hog Farms, where they are Dumped Out and Eaten Up, without anyone knowing anything about it, including the Robot Engineer who Drives the Train and Dumps Out the Boxcars.

Yes, it was a Practical Mechanical Thing to do during the early 1940's; but, Adolf Hitler did not Think of it: beCause he did not Intend to Murder his Jewish SLAVES, whom he Worked in his Factories. For Example, Auschwitz was a Work Camp for making Kerosene Fuel for Jet Airplanes, which was made from Coal, which Explains WHY so many Boxcars of Coal were coming into the Camp, which did not have any Gas Chambers, and which only had 2 Crematoriums with 3 Ovens, each, which was Documented by Russian Surveillance Cameras in Spy Airplanes, which flew over the Camp, almost Daily, which Cameras Photographed everything that went on there from an Eagle's Perspective, whereby it can easily be Proven in a Courtroom that there were no thousand Jews Cremated Daily, nor even 100 of them: beCause it Requires no less than 4 Hours to Cremate just one Tiny Adult Body, even Today. Indeed, it Requires no less than one Hour, just to Heat Up the Retort, and 2 to 10 Hours to Cremate the Body at 4000 °F, and then at least one more Hour to Cool Off the Oven before the Door can be Safely Opened! †§‡

Z-[_] It is now Obvious that there are Outlandish LIES in the HoloHOAX Museum, in the District of Criminals, in Washington, which has Placards stating that 4 to 5 Bodies were put into one Oven every 10 Minutes, as if that were Physically Possible! Therefore, those Zebras should be brought to Court in Shackles and Chains, and be Forced to Prove it, or else be Stuffed into Crematory Ovens, which is what King Nebuchadnezzar would do with them. (See *the Book of Daniel* for the Proof.) †§‡

05-03 [_] O Adolf, I can now Understand WHY the Germans Loved you, and were Willing to Die for you: beCause you are an Honest Person, while those Lying Edomites are the most Corrupt Selfish GREEDY Sons of Satan who ever Lived! Moreover, whomever Disagrees with that is Suspect of being Anti-American, and should be Watched by the FBI and CIA. †§‡

05-04 [_] Well, I have always said that those Lying Edomites are Untrustworthy People, or else they would DEMAND: **"The Great Worldwide TELEVISED Court HEARING!"** **(That Great Meeting of the Most Intelligent and Well-Educated Minds!) By The Worldwide People's Revolution!®**, Book 041, just to Learn the Whole Truth about a LOT of Important Subjects — such as WHO Assassinated President Kennedy? Yes, if they were Honest Upright Trustworthy Citizens, they would be the First to DEMAND that Great Meeting of the Most Intelligent Minds, which would Naturally Include the Selected King of **The Worldwide People's Revolution!®**, who is perhaps the Most Honest Man among us, who would Do what is RIIT for ALL of us, if he were in Charge of Things in this World of Wonders, which has no Lack of Mountains of Rocks to Work with, whereby everyone in the World can have a Beautiful Stone Dome Home Complex to Live in, which is Self-air-conditioned, Fireproof, Hail-proof, Tornado-proof, Insurance-proof, Mouse-proof, Termite-proof, Rot-proof, Paint-proof, and Tax-proof: beCause of being Built like the PANTHEON in Rome. (See *Wikipedia* for the Proof.) Yes, it is now Physically Possible for **"Seven Great Armies of Working Soldiers!"** **(HOW to Provide a Way for Everyone to WORK: so as to Eliminate Poverty, Crimes, Drug Abuses, Prisons and Unnecessary Taxes!)**, Book 015, to Build those **"GLORIOUS Swanky Hotels Castles and Fortresses!"** **(Beautiful Planned City States for WISE Intelligent Well-Educated People with Common Sense and Good Understanding!)**, Book 019, by Exercising our DUMBmocracy, whereby we can VOTE for the Establishment of: **"The New RIGHTEOUS**

One-World Government!" (HOW to Establish a Righteous One-World Government without Going to WAR!), Book 056, which should be Established in: **"The Great World TEMPLE of PEACE!" (The Glory of Jerusalem Arises Again!)**, Book 017, which will be the Tallest and Largest Building in the World, being no less than 8 Miles in Diameter and nearly a Mile High, being Built UP in 60 Great Terraces, having 10 Minor Terraces in each Great Terrace, having Beautiful Stone Dome Home Complexes within the Terraces, having Gardens, Vineyards and Orchards Planted on the Roofs of them: so that the Elected Leaders of the Nations can get up and go to Work at HOME, or near Home, along with their Voluntary Servants, who will all get to Live in those Palaces, Free of Charges, which will be their Just Compensations for their Services, which Leaders will Collect Lower Wages than Dishwashers and Gardeners at Swanky Fortresses: beCause all of their Expenses will be Covered. †§‡ {See: **"A List of FAIR Swanky Wages!" (The Equitable Wage System!) By The Worldwide People's Revolution!®** Book 065.}

05-05 [_] Are you saying, O Adolf, that the Elected Leaders of the Nations will have to do their own Gardening, Cooking, Clothes Making, Cleaning Houses, and everything? Will they also have to Build their own Beautiful Stone Dome Home Complexes within Swanky Fortresses?

05-06 [_] No, but I am saying that each Potential Elected Leader will have to Fill Out and File the Complete SURVEYS of their VALUES on the Internet for everyone to Study: so that the Electors might know WHO to Vote for: beCause no more Election Deceptions are Required for True Prosperity. Moreover, I am saying that there is **"A Sound Argument for Masters and Servants!" (WHY Everyone Needs a Good Master, and every Master Needs Good Obedient Servants!) By The Worldwide People's Revolution!®** Book 008. Therefore, those Voluntary Servants of those Elected Officials will do their Gardening, House Cleaning, Cooking, Clothes Making, and whatever their Masters Want them to Do. Indeed, which ones of the following Boxes would you Check with an X, which might Prove whether or not you were Born to be a Master or a Servant?

> A-[_] I Agree that no Election Deceptions are Necessary for True Prosperity: beCause there is no Lack of Mountains of Rocks for **"Seven Great Armies of Working Soldiers"** to Work with, who may use the Best of the Latest Technologies and Equipment for doing their Work Properly with Well-made Tools, even as if they were going to War, to WIN.

> B-[_] I have already Bought into the Idea, and I LOVE the Sound of it! Yes, just Imagine what **"The Swanky Associations of Working Soldiers,"** (Book 018), could Accomplish if they had an Unlimited Supply of Good Money to Work with, and Well-make Tools to Work with, whereby they could Construct those **"GLORIOUS Swanky Hotels Castles and Fortresses!"** with the Greatest of Ease — which just Happen to have more than 5,000 Advantages over normal Cities of Confusion, which must be Emphasized, or Repeated, over and over: beCause most People Fail to get that Message into their Brains. For Example, there is no Need for any Cars, Buses, Trucks, Lawnmowers, Weed-eaters, Motorboats, Garden Tillers, Snow Blowers, Noisy Motorcycles, nor any other Noisy STINKING Polluting Abominations, which will Save us Trillions of Dollars, while Cleaning up the Atmosphere, Water, and Land, while also Raising our Standard of Living by many Degrees. {See www.Amazon.com for: **"The Right Design for Living!" (A List of Great Advantages for Building Beautiful Planned City States!)**, Book 012.}

C-[_] I Confess that it would be a Vast Improvement over our Present Lifestyles.

D-[_] No Dimwitcrat would Check the C-Box: beCause of not being Humble enough to Confess that we have been Living WRong, whereby we have Produced tens of millions of Criminals, Drug Addicts, Gluttons, FAT Hogs, and Proud Roosters, who get up in Congress and BOAST about the Greatness of America, which Consumes no less than 20 Million Barrels of Oil each Day, on Average, and has nothing Constructive to Show for it, except some more Capitalist TRASH, Endless DEBTS, Polluted Cities, and Trash Dumps FULL of Litter and Stink! Indeed, what Kind of Kingdom of GOD is that? †§‡

E-[_] Educated People already know that it is Possible and most Practical to Build Beautiful Planned City States — except that Lying Edomites would not Approve of them, unless they could make the Masses of People into their Low-paid SLAVES.

F-[_] I Fail to Understand WHY you are Picking on those Lying Edomites, O Adolf? †§‡

G-[_] God knows that your Brains are Malfunctioning, if you cannot Understand that NO Slavery is Needed for having TRUE Prosperity: beCause we have Mechanical Slaves for doing most of the Difficult Work. Therefore, to Help you to Understand, my Adopted Son has written this Inspired Book for you to Study. Therefore, do not Think nor Speak Evil of him: beCause he is a GOOD Person, who Fears God and Loves Provable Truths. ‡

H-[_] Honest People already Confess that our Selected King has the Best Solutions for our Massive Problems. However, Wicked Politicians Deny it.

I-[_] I Checked the H-Box with an X: because it is True. Moreover, if anyone does not Check the H-Box, such a Person is Suspect of being an Edomite Lover, rather than an Israelite Lover: beCause, even Jesus Christ, himself, would Check the H-Box: beCause his Holy Spirit Inspired the Wonderful Books of our Selected King, including this one! Yes, it can easily be Proven in a Courtroom that they are Inspired by GOD, himself. †§‡

J-[_] Justice Demands that we Prove it in a Courtroom, and Publish the Evidences to all of the People in the World, in all Major Languages: so that they might Discover HOW to Solve their Massive Problems without the Assistance of any Bloodthirsty Lying Edomites, who will Speak Evil of that Great Meeting of the Most Intelligent Minds! †§‡

K-[_] King Jesus would Love it. Yes, just Imagine if you were Looking Down on this World of Woes from the Sky, from God's Point of View, and thus Saw what a Horrible Condition it is now in — Thanks mostly to Capitalism — would you not VOTE for the Establishment of **"The New RIGHTEOUS One-World Government!"**? Of course you would, if you were a God of True JUSTICE; but, if you were a Lying Snake, like Bernie Madoff, you would only be Thinking of HOW you might Profit from it, Personally. †§‡

L-[_] Lots of Laughs! King Jesus is not the Slightest Bit Interested in Establishing Peace nor True Prosperity on this Earth: beCause he Loves VIOLENCE, Destructions, Wars, Crimes, Drugs, Hospitals, MediSINZ, and all of the Wonderful Things that make this

World a Heavenly Place to Live! Yes, *"The LORD is a Man of War,"* even as it is Revealed in *Exodus 15:3*. {See www.Amazon.com for: **"The Environmentalists' Paradise!" (HOW almost Everyone could be Living in a Beautiful Manmade Paradise!) By The Worldwide People's Revolution!®** Book 035.} †§‡§§

M-[_] My Instincts tell me that most People will say and do almost anything **"For the Love of Money!" (The Strange Things that People Say and Do to Get more Money!)**, Book 003. Yes, if you Doubt it, just Ask George Warmonger Bush, Incorporated, which includes Condoosleezee Rice Patty, Paul Wolfwits, Henry "Hank" Paul's Son, Robert Covered-up Oklahoma City Bombing Mueller, Donald Rummy Fell, Big Dick Chicanery, John Lightning Strikes Bolton, and a whole List of Chief Criminals, who are Black-Listed in one of our Selected King's Inspired Books, who should be getting Prepared for: **"The Great Worldwide TELEVISED Court HEARING!"** Book 041. †§‡

N-[_] Not everyone likes to read such a LONG Introduction, O Adolf. Can you not Discover an Editor?

O-[_] There is an Option. Yes, you could read *The Adventures of Huck Finn and Nigger Jim,* who could tell you all about that Education Slavery, Work Slavery, Tax Slavery, Interest Slavery, Insurance Slavery, Drug Slavery, Sex Slavery, and ElecTrickery Bills Slavery, when it is Possible and most Practical for everyone to be FREE with a Capital F, having NO Bills at all to Pay: beCause of Obeying **"The New MAGNIFIED Version of the 20 Commandments!"** See: **"LIGHTNING STRIKES Versus Lightning Bugs!" (HOW you can Become Moderately RICH, without Telling any Lies nor Selling any Trash!) By The Worldwide People's Revolution!®** Book 074. †§‡ {See also: **"UNLIMITED ENERJEE 99 Percent Pollutions Free!"** Book 029.}

P-[_] It is not Possible to have NO Bills to Pay, unless you want to Live in a CAVE with King David. (See *First Samuel 22:1, KJV.*) †§‡

Q-[_] The Great Question is this: **"Are you People Willing to take it to COURT, and Prove whether or not it is Possible to Live without any Bills to Pay?"** Well, the remainder of this Inspired Book will Help you to Understand that Plan.

R-[_] I am Restricted by my Ignorance and Reluctance, and have no Idea what you are Talking about, O Adolf. Indeed, this whole Book is nothing but a Mystery to me: beCause I do not Know WHO you are.

S-[_] Well, that is only beCAUSE you have Failed to Study my Son's Previous Book, called: **"The Loathsome Burdens of the Independent Jackasses!" (A New Approach for Solving our Massive Problems!) By The Leader — Adolf Dictator Hitler, Junior!** Book 051.

T-[_] It is Time to take a Break: beCause all of this Information is getting too Heavy on my Mind. In Fact, my Head is about to EXPLODE with TNT (Technological Nasty Terminologies), if you know what I Mean? †§‡

U-[_] I Understand what you Mean; but, whenever you Want to take a Break, all you have to do is Mark the Page Number and Verse with a Bookmarker, where you may take up your Study, later on — except that it is always Best to read an entire Book during just one Day, while it is Fresh in your Mind: so as to Eliminate any Confusion of Thoughts. †

V-[_] I find it Valuable to Finish at least one whole Chapter of any Book, and to Finish the whole Book within at least one Week. However, this is one of those little Books that can easily be Finished in just one or 2 Days. Therefore, try to make an Appointment with it, with that Thought in Mind, to Finish it during just one or 2 Days, even if you have to Hide yourself in the Woods, somewhere with a Lawn Chair that stretches out, and is Comfortable. Yes, take your Pillow along with you, just in case you might also need some Sleep: beCause it is Good to be Wide Awake when you read any Inspired Book, which has a Tendency to Relax the Reader, and thus put him or her to Sleep, whereby you might get more out of it when you Wake Up and Continue Reading. †‡

W-[_] Wicked People have no Interest in Reproving themselves by Reading any such Books, which is WHY you will never See People like George Warmonger Bush reading them, even with a lower-case r, which is without any Enthusiasm. †‡

X-[_] X-amount of Poor People will Love this Inspired Book, and will do their Best to Spread the Good News that can be found in it, even though there is a much Better one, called: **"The UGLY Scarred Dishonest Face of Poor Old Miserable UNCLE SAM!" (A Memorial Day Legacy!) By The Worldwide People's Revolution!®** Book 054. Indeed, Amazon dot UK (United Kingdom) Offers the first 24 Pages for Free in their Book Preview: because they Recognize the Beauty of it, being more Intelligent People. †

Y-[_] That might have been True in Yesteryears, when People were not Distracted by Televisions, Radios and Telephones; but, nowadays, hardly anyone finds the Time to Read anything Properly, which is SLOWLY and Carefully, 2 or 3 Times, minimum. ‡

Z-[_] Honest Zoo Keepers know that not everyone is Alike; but, each Creature is Unique and Special, which is also True of Good Books, which must also be Educational, Entertaining, Enlightening, and Enjoyable — and much more Readable than the *Old Testament,* which has certain Parts that one could say are LOATHSOME, which might Explain WHY it is seldom Studied, nowadays. However, the Author of this Inspired Book has Changed all of that, and has made it much more Readable. {See the Internet on www.Amazon.com for: **"Thu Nq MAGNUFIID Verzhun uv Thu PROVERBZ uv KING SOLUMUN in Plaan Ingglish!" (The Understandable Version of the Famous Proverbs of King Solomon in Plain English!) By The Worldwide People's Revolution!®,** Book 028, plus: **"ECCLESIASTES UNCOVERED!" (The New MAGNIFIED Version of Ecclesiastes and the Song of Solomon in Plain English!),** Book 034, which is only Surpassed by: **"The New MAGNIFIED Version of The Book of MORMON!" (The Story of the White and Dark Indians in the Americas!),** Book 040, which comes in 2 Volumes of about 500 Pages, each, which will provide a Lifetime of Education, Entertainment, Enlightenment, and Enjoyable Reading. Nevertheless, I Prefer **"The New MAGNIFIED Version of ISAIAH in Plain English!" (The Understandable Version of the Book of Isaiah!) By The Worldwide People's**

(HOW to be Liberated from all Slavery, Worldwide!)

Revolution!® Book 044. Moreover, you could hardly Discover Literature that is Better than **"The New MAGNIFIED Version of the GOOD NEWS According to Saint LUKE!" (The Magnified Gospel of Saint Luke in Plain English!)**, Book 061, which is only Surpassed by: **"The New MAGNIFIED Version of the GOOD NEWS According to Saint JOHN!" (The Gospel According to Saint John Zebedee Boanerges in Plain English!)**, Book 062, which is Greatly Enhanced by **"The New MAGNIFIED Version of the PSALMS of King David!" (The Understandable Version of the Famous Psalms in Plain English!)**, Book 064, which is a Masterpiece of Fine Literature! ‡

05-07 [_] O Adolf, it seems to me that there is nothing so LOATHSOME in the Line of Literature, in this World of Wonders, as the Unholy Mutilated Bible, which could make a Person SICK, just to read it with an Honest Mind. For Example, there is that Noah's Ark Story, which makes it out that Noah actually Managed to Feed and Water no less than 8 Million Species of Creatures, most of which are Insects — such as a Million or more Species of ANTS, which can be found all over the World, which would not have Survived for 14 Months in the Ark: beCause there was no Fresh Water Supply, nor was there any Way that only 8 People could have Cleaned up, after the 28,000+ Bovines Pooped and Pissed all over it and themselves. Indeed, many Professing "Christians" have no Idea just how MANY Deers, Goats, Sheeps, and Different Kinds of Cattles there are in this World of Wonders. For Example, there are well over a thousand Kinds of Deers, Sheeps, Goats and Antelopes, most of which have gone Extinct. Nevertheless, there are hundreds of Kinds still Alive. Therefore, if Noah got 7 Males and 7 Females of each Clean Beast into the Ark, including all Bovines, Deers, Antelopes, Goats, Mountain Sheeps, Yaks, Musk Oxens, Reindeers, Caribous, Mooses, Elks, Bisons, Water Buffaloes, Giraffes, and so on, that would be no less than 14 of each Kind, which would Drink up no less than 20 Gallons of Fresh Water per Day, each, times 28,000, and would Equal no less than 560,000 Gallons of Water just for the Bovines, Deers, Antelopes, Sheeps, and Goats, etc. — not Counting the Camels, Rhinos, Hippopotamuses, Zebras, Asses, Elephants, Kudus, Llamas, Alpacas, Guanacos, Vicunas, Gazelles, Horses, Black Bears, Brown Bears, Polar Bears, Pandas, Giant Pandas, Red Pandas, Shrews, Lions, Tigers, Leopards, Cheetahs, Jaguars, Panthers, Hamsters, Salamanders, Rabbits, Kangaroos, Wallabies, Koalas, Komodo Dragons, Lizards, Sloths, Snails, Spiders, Wolverines, Dogs, Laughing Hyenas, Jackals, Hogs, Foxes, Wolves, Coyotes, Skinks, Skunks, Minks, Moles, Porcupines, Prairie Dogs, Mongooses, Mice, Rats, Snakes, Raccoons, Opossums, Squirrels, Chipmunks, Okapis, Gerbils, Meer Cats, Ferrets, Bearcats, Anteaters, Aardvarks, Tapirs, Tarsiers, Groundhogs, Armadillos, Badgers, Barracudas, Otters, Bats, Beavers, Bees, Termites, Butterflies, Countless Monkeys, Apes, Mountain Gorillas, Baboons, Chimpanzees, Kangaroos, Koala Bears, Wallabies, Wasps, Weasels, Geese, Swans, Chickens, Guinea Fowls, Guinea Pigs, Ducks, Penguins, Pigeons, Cranes, Crows, Herons, Hornets, Ravens, Doves, Pheasants, Peacocks, Prairie Chickens, Guinea Fowls, Turkeys, Flamingos, Hawks, Owls, Eagles, Falcons, Vultures, Sea Gulls, Pelicans, Robbins, Finches, Sparrows, Bluejays, Cardinals, Blue Birds, Black Birds, Yellow Birds, Pink Birds, Red Birds, Gray Birds, Speckled Birds, White Birds, and so on — even no less than 100,000 Species of them! Therefore, how many Tanks of Water did Noah have in the Ark, since just one 560,000-gallon Water Tank would take up a HUGE Space, bigger than most American Houses? Yes, just Multiply it Times 300 Days, and you have no less than 168,000,000,000 Gallons of Water, or enough to Fill 400 Arks, without any Exaggerations! And what about the 35 Million Bails of Hay for all of those Beasts to Eat? Who could Handle all of them within one Year, after Butchering all of the Beeves for the Carnivores to Eat? †§‡§§

05-08 [_] Well, I have been saying for several Years that all such Things should be Proven in a Courtroom to the whole World, whereby all such Unholy Books can either be Corrected, or BURNED: beCause we have Heard enough Lies for one Lifetime! †§‡

05-09 [_] O Adolf, you would Surely NOT Burn the *Holy Bible,* would you?

05-10 [_] NO! — not if it were Actually HOLY; but, it at least Appears to be another Lying Edomite FABRICATION of the Devil, himself: beCause it can Rightly be Blamed for most of the Troubles in this World of Woes, which my Adopted Son, Adolf Hitler, Junior, will Explore in this Marvelous Book, and Hopefully get the Record Straight. After all, without the Assistance of Satan, the Devil, HOW would those Lying Edomites have ever Accomplished what they have Accomplished for themselves, whereby they are now Registered in the Courts of Heaven as those LYING Rich Bloodthirsty RED Hairy Edomites, who are the Descendants of that very Hairy Esau? — that is, IF the Angel Gabriel has Informed me Correctly; and, I Sincerely Believe that he has! †§‡

— Chapter 06 —

Adolf Hitler Junior takes up his Unholy Mutilated Bible!

06-01 [_] I Refuse to read any farther. You have Crossed the Line, O Adolf.

06-02 [_] My Curiosity has Overcome me. Therefore, I will continue to Read this Book.

06-03 [_] I have already heard enough lies for one day. However, if I had to make a List of all such Lies, and Present them to a Judge in a Courtroom, I would find myself to be most Ashamed: beCause, for some Strange Reason, I cannot Discover so much as ONE Provable Lie in this Book. †§‡

06-04 [_] I Hate to Admit it, even as most People in America will likely Hate to Confess it; but, the Inspired Author of this Unique Book deserves to be Heard: beCause he makes some Valid Points, which should not be Ignored. For Example, can any Honest American Rightly DENY that most Americans Live in Firetrap Houses, which are Subject to Blowing Away, if not Burning Up? Indeed, the Statistics Reveal that hundreds of thousands of American "Homes" are Destroyed each Year by Fires, Floods, Tornadoes, Hurricanes, Termites, Dry Rot, and Wrecking Balls: beCause they are Obviously Designed by Lying Edomites, who LOVE the Insurance Money that is Collected from Ignorant FOOLS, which Amounts to no less than a Trillion Dollars per Year, for Houses that could have been Loan-proof, Interest-proof, Mortgage-proof, Self-air-conditioned, Fireproof, Tornado-proof, Hurricane-proof, Mouse-proof, Termite-proof, Rot-proof, Paint-proof, Earthquake-proof, Insurance-proof, and Tax-proof! Yes, the PANTHEON in Rome is the Perfect Example for us to Study. †‡ (See *Wikipedia* for *Pantheon / Building.*)

06-05 [_] I put my Red X in Box 06-04: beCause it is telling the TRUTH.

(HOW to be Liberated from all Slavery, Worldwide!)

A-[_] I Wasted 5,000+ dollars, just last year, Heating and Cooling my almost Worthless Wooden / Plastic Firetrap House, in Anaheim, Californicate.

B-[_] I Believe that I Wasted 4,000+$ for Insurance for my House and Car, just last Year. (Please write in below the Amount of Money that you Spent on your House and Vehicle for Needless Insurance for the Past 10 Years, seeing that Swanky Fortresses use only Electric Elevators and Subway Trains for Transportation, which alone have more than a thousand Advantages over Cities of Confusion.)

C-[_] I Confess that I Waste 4,000+$, on Average per Year, for Repairs for my House and Vehicle: beCause I do not Live in a Beautiful Planned City State.

D-[_] DUMBmocracy never Informed us that there was any other Way to Live. Yes, we can Blame that onto those Lying Deceiving Edomites, who Control the News Media and Public Schools.

E-[_] Educated People have known it all along; but, few of them could ever Afford to Build their own Private Pantheons, much less their own Private Trillion-dollar Swanky Fortresses. However, the Money that was Wasted by Americans on Houses, Highways, Cars, Trucks, Buses, Mobile Homes, Motorcycles, Lawnmowers, Drugs, Insurance, Gasoline, Repair Bills, Paints, Cosmetics, Telephones, Televisions, and Needless Toys, has already been enough Money to have Built Beautiful Swanky Fortresses for everyone in the World! †§‡

F-[_] I Fail to Understand how else we could Live. We have to have Cars to get to Work. We have to have Trucks to Transport our Foods and Goods. And therefore, we have to have Highways, Vehicles, Insurance, Taxes, Hospitals, Medical Doctors, and every single Thing that we now have, just to make our Lives Functional. Period. †§‡

G-[_] God knows that you need to Study all of the Inspired Books by the Man with the Spirit of Elijah.

H-[_] Hi, this is Huck Finn, and I did not Learn how to Read nor Write. Therefore, what am I supposed to Do to make myself Healthy and Happy?

I-[_] Ignorant People like you need to go to some School of Fools, and Learn HOW. {See www.Amazon.com for: **"The Public School of IGNERUNT FQLZ!" (HOW we have been GRAATLEE DISEEVD by Capitalism!)**, Book 024, which will Teach to you how to "Reed and Riit" within short order.}

J-[_] Judge Thatcher would Disagree with that Plan: because there would not be enough Criminals in his Courtroom to keep him Busy. †§

K-[_] King Jesus would Love it, seeing that he was Contented to be Free, Healthy, and Happy, without any American Trash, much less the Trainloads of Capitalist Trash that comes to America from China, whose People are Greatly Suffering with Chronic

Constipation of their Minds, who should have Consulted with our Selected King before Building or Making anything: because now they have just Wasted the past 30 Years on Vanities — except that they have also Greatly Polluted themselves with Stinking Noisy Vehicles: beCause of Copying the Great False American Edomite Economy. †§‡

L-[_] Lots of Laughs! King Jesus has no use for reading books. He never even went to School to Learn anything: beCause he was God, himself! †§‡§§

M-[_] If there were enough Money involved, most Lying Edomites would also Love it: beCause they Love whatever is Profitable, even if it Causes Cancers. Indeed, there was a Time in American History when the Advertisers of Cigarettes said that Medical Doctors Recommended Smoking for Good Health; and those were Edomite Medical Doctors. †§‡

06-06 [_] But, it is not telling the WHOLE Truth: beCause there is no such a Thing as a Flood-proof Earthquake-proof House. In Fact, the Pantheon has been Flooded many Times during the past 2,000 or so Years, and was even Burned to the Ground one Time, before General Hadrian Reconstructed it with ROCKS, which have been there for no less than 1,800 Years as a Mute Testimony that our Selected King is CORRECT! †§‡§§

06-07 [_] You are very Sarcastic, which is Permissible in all Adolf Dictator Hitler Junior Literature, just as long as it is made Perfectly Clear that it is the Tale of a SNAKE. For Example, I Seriously Doubt that the Pantheon has ever been Flooded, since Rome sits on 7 Hills, and is not down in some Swamp of Filthiness like Washington, District of Corruption. †§‡

06-08 [_] Are you not Aware that Rome is one of the most Evil Places on this Earth, being Surpassed only by New Yuck City, Houston Texas, Dallas-Fort Worthless, Lost Wages Nevada, Lost Angels Californicate, Hong Kong, Moscow, Lungdung, Berlin, and Paris? †§‡

06-09 [_] Well, I have no Way to Measure the Corruption of any given City; but, I would say that they are ALL Corrupt to some Degree: beCause it is just the Nature of Hordes of People to get themselves Corrupted when they Depart from the Land, and take up the Occupations of Lying Edomites — such as Bankercraft, whereby Rich Edomite Bankers have Awarded themselves with Million-dollar Bonuses for being "Good Stewards of God's Money," which all Belongs to them — at least according to the *Holy Bible*, which clearly states: *"Blest are the Lying Edomites: beCause they will Inherit the True Riches, of Silver, Gold, Platinum, Diamonds, Rubies, Emeralds, Sapphires, Pearls, Onyxes, Marbles, Granites, and other Precious Things from the Bowels of the Good Earth: beCause they are my Chosen People, says the Most High God. However, I am being Extremely Sarcastic: beCause no such Lying Snakes will have any Inheritance in the Holy Kingdom of All that is Good: beCause it is Prepared for the Riichus Ones, who do what is Riit for themselves and others, including their Animals, who have an Equal Right to Live a Natural Life, and not as just another Slave of some Cruel Master, who Vainly Imagines that he will not have a Judgment Day, just beCause he is another Lying Edomite, who is Supposedly Exempt from True Justice, who Thinks of other People as being Beasts, and even Snakes, when he is the Lying Snake, himself! Yes, it is a Shame on him, which is brought on him by his Pride, whereby he Vainly Imagines that he is of some Superior Race, who have Special Blessings from some God, who Identified himself as JEHOVAH God, which the Translators of* *the Gay King James Version (KJV) called the LORD God, as in Lord Mountbatten, who was the Uncle of Prince Philip of Great Britain. Indeed, the British Peoples have had many Lords and a few Saviors; but, none of them were quite as Powerful as the LORD God of Israel, who was a Man of War, according to the Unholy Mutilated Bible, which Promotes those Useless Wars, which even an Idiot could Understand is WRong: beCause nothing could be more Hateful nor Needless than Wars. Therefore, Wise People would figure out HOW to get around having them: beCause they are just a Total Waste of Healthy Young Flesh, which should be at Home in Bed with some other Healthy Young Flesh when Night comes: beCause the Whole Objective is to Produce HOLY Children, which can only be Produced from HOLY Parents, who have Purified their Minds and Bodies by Means of much Fasting and Praying and Eating Correctly between Fasts. Yes, that might Sound Strange to you Ignorant People, who have never 'red' the Bible so much as one Time from Cover to Cover, whereby you did not Discover the many Verses about Fasting. For Example, in Deuteronomy 9, you can read about Moses going up on Mount Sinai, where he Fasted for 40 Days and 40 Nights without Eating nor Drinking, which you might find Unbelievable, even as I find it Unbelievable in most Bibles. However, the Part about him taking Daily Enemas with Pure Water was Deleted by those Lying Edomites, which Enemas were Administered by Joshua, his Faithful Friend. Yes, he Packed the Water up the Mountain for Moses; but, not for Drinking: beCause he went Dry, except for those Enemas and Baths. Likewise, the whole City of Nineveh Fasted and Prayed for 40 Nights and 40 Days, while they took Enemas whenever they Needed them, even as Jonah Instructed them, whereby they Survived the 'Ordeal,' you might say. However, most People would not Believe it, much less Study: **'The Gospel According to our Elected King!' (The Good News from the Most Modern Perspective!) By The Worldwide People's Revolution!®**, Book 077, which should be Mandatory Reading in all Churches, Mosques, Synagogues, Temples, Cathedrals, and Basilicas, Worldwide: beCause only the Whole Truth has the Power to Liberate you People from your Prison of Lies and Sins."* — NMV {See www.Amazon.com for the above Book, plus: **"HOW to Become a HOLY Man!" (40 Good Reasons WHY People Should FAST and PRAY!)**, Book 045, plus: **"The Proper RULES for FASTING!" (The Complete Instruction Manual for True Repentance!) By The Worldwide People's Revolution!®** Book 046.}

06-10 [_] O Adolf Junior, that is no Quotation from any Bible.

— Chapter 07 —

The Greatest Sin is the Rejection of Truths!

07-01 [_] Most Professing "Christians" are not Aware that they are Sinning most every Day, even if they Live according to their Religious Beliefs: beCause their Beliefs are WRong in most Cases, which has already been Explained in: **"What is WRong with those Professing Christians?" (A Self-Examination of the Heart of the Body of Good Government!)**, Book 002, which is a Companion Book of: **"What is WRong with those CRAZY Christians?" By The Worldwide People's Revolution!®**, Book 076, which contains many Photographs with Explanations. Yes, some of them make their Daily Confessions: beCause of Falling from Grace, you might say. Little do they Know the Cure for whatever Ails them. Little do they Know that the One and ONLY Way OUT of the Prison of Lies and Deceptions is to pass through the Doorway of Confession, which is the Beginning of Enlightenment.

07-02 [_] O Adolf Dictator Hitler, Junior, are you going to Instruct us about the Ways of Righteousness, when your own "Father" was one of the most Vile Men who ever Lived, who Murdered more than 6,000,000 Jews — most of whom were Honest White Jews, who Suffered for the Sins of Lying Edomites? Indeed, if Adolf Hitler could have somehow SEPARATED the Honest White Jews from the Lying Edomites, he would not have been found so Guilty in the Eyes of Jehovah God, who would most Certainly Separate the Good People from the Bad People: beCause it is not Right to Condemn the Just with the Unjust. †§‡

07-03 [_] Well, I Agree 100% with some of what you say. However, you do not have your so-called "Facts" Straight. First of all, my Father never Murdered even ONE Honest White Jew, nor even one Lying Edomite: beCause, if there was any Murdering going on, it was done by Lying Edomites, who called themselves "Zionists," who Constructed the Concentration Camps, and also Managed them, which you can Discover on YouTube Videos, which needs to be Proven at: **"The Great Worldwide TELEVISED Court HEARING,"** along with all other Related Subjects, including what Actually Happened in those Concentration Camps. †‡

07-04 [_] O Adolf, there are always at least 2 Sides to every Story, and sometimes 3 or 4 Sides — Depending on WHO you Listen to. However, those Lying Edomites made Graveyard Mistakes, whereby they Published millions of books with Outlandish Lies in them, which can easily be Proven in a Courtroom. For Example, their Books say that "there were 2 great smoking chimneys at Auschwitz," which supposedly Vented the Smoke from no less than 30 Crematory Ovens! Yes, it would be Extremely Difficult to Vent more than 3 such Furnaces in one Chimney, unless it was a HUGE Chimney, which neither one of them was, which have been Photographed hundreds of Times by the Russian Surveillance / Reconnaissance Cameras, which Photos clearly show the SIZE of each Chimney, which were Large Chimneys; but, they were not 20 feet in Diameter, as they would have had to have been to Accommodate so many Ovens. Moreover, getting the Smoke from one End of a Building to the other End of it from a Hot Retort would present its own Special Problem: beCause Heat and Smoke like to RISE UP. Therefore, so much Smoke would be Choking OUT the Fires: beCause of a Lack of Proper Ventilation, which can be

Proven in a Courtroom for whomever might Doubt it. Indeed, I Certainly do NOT Doubt it: beCause I used to have a Stove with a Long Stovepipe on it, which ran into a Brick Chimney: beCause I Calculated that much of the Heat was simply going UP the Chimney, when it should be going into the Room. Therefore, I installed a Long Stovepipe on the Wood-and-Coal-burning Stove, only to Discover that it did not Vent very well: beCause the Smoke was Trapped in the Long Stovepipe, which often sent Smoke into the Room through the Joints of the Pipe — at least until the Fire got to Burning Well, which almost always Required a lot of Time, when Compared with a Normal Fireplace, which Vents straight up into the Chimney. Therefore, I do not Swallow the Edomite Lie about 15 Crematory Ovens being Vented by just one Chimney, when all such Ovens are Heated by HUGE Fires, just to get them up to 4000 °F / 2204 °C. Moreover, all such Fires have to be Smothered Out before the Ovens can be Cooled Off enough to Safely Open the Doors on them, which Requires at least one Hour, if the Weather is Cool. However, in the Case of Auschwitz, the Weather was not always Cool; and therefore, it might have Required 2 Hours or more to Cool Off such Hot Ovens. †§‡

07-05 [_] Well, I Sincerely Believe that we can Discover the WHOLE Truth about it at: **"The Great Worldwide TELEVISED Court HEARING!"** Book 041. However, in the Meantime, if anyone can Present any Contrary "Facts" about it, I would like to Hear them.

07-06 [_] O Adolf, there is a really Good Chance that Scientists will Agree with you: beCause you seem to have the True Facts on your Side. However, that is not to say that there was NO Holocaust, is it?

07-07 [_] Well, there were Certainly a LOT of People who Died during World War 2 — somewhere around 60 Million, and most of them were NOT in any Nazi Prison Camps, whom I Prefer to Honor as the VICTIMS of Capitalism and Communism, which were Isms of Lying Edomites, which can also be Proven in a Courtroom, if anyone is Interested. Indeed, some of the Capitalist and Communist Ideas come from the Unholy Mutilated Bible, itself! Yes, you can read about "Commonism" in *The Book of the Acts of the Apostles,* which follows *the Gospel according to Saint John Zebedee Boanerges,* which is one of my Favorite Books — that is, in the New MAGNIFIED Version (NMV), which is at least twice as long as the KJV, and 10 Times as Good. However, that is not to say that the Victims of Concentration Camps do not Deserve any Honor: because I am Sure that many of them were as Innocent as most Jews, Today, who likely have no Idea what their Edomite "Brothers" are up to. After all, it is not something that is Taught in **"The Public School of IGNERUNT FQLZ!" (HOW we have been GRAATLEE DISEEVD by Capitalism!)**, Book 024, which is a Companion Book of: **"The BIG White OUTHOUSE on the Not-so-Biblical Capitol DUNGHILL!" (The Chief Sins of the Divided States of United Lies!)**, Book 023. †§‡

07-08 [_] O Adolf, the First Church of Christ was certainly NOT Communists by any Means, even though they did have *"all things in common,"* whatever that Means, which our Selected King has already Explained in one of his Good Books, which Reveals that they Shared their Wealth, and Certainly did NOT Practice Capitalism, whereby they soon Died Out: beCause they did not take Advantage of other People, like Capitalist Hogs do, who will Say and Do almost anything for Gain: beCause they are Baal Worshipers, or Possession Worshipers, whom God HATES more than any other Worshipers of Idols: beCause such Greedy People can and do

Murder other People, in order to Obtain their Possessions, which is normally what Inspires Wars, as the Apostle James explained to some degree. Whatever the Case, almost every Family on this Earth has *"all things in common among them"*: beCause it is the only Way that such a Family can Live Together in Peace. Indeed, just Imagine how a Wife would Feel, if her Husband kept all of the Money that he Earned for himself, and did not Share any Money with her? Moreover, what would the Children Think of such Selfishness? Could they Respect their Father? Furthermore, if they could not Respect him, HOW could they Love him? Therefore, it is a Normal Thing for Husbands to Sacrifice everything for their Wives and Children, while their Wives Sacrifice their Lives to make their Homes Welcoming to their Husbands, who come Home very Tired, after Slaving away all Day to Earn a Living and Pay the Bills, which the First Church of Christ never had to Deal with: beCause they Lived Simple Lives, and were Contented with Foods and Clothing, just as the Apostle Paul Explained in *First Timothy 6*. †§‡

07-09 [_] Well, our Selected King has a much Better Version of *First Timothy 6* in: **"For the Love of Money!" (The Strange Things that People Say and Do to Get more Money!)**, Book 003. Whatever the First Church of Jesus Christ Actually did is not Explained in the Bible: beCause it is a Mutilated Book, which has many of the most Precious Parts Removed by those Lying Edomites, who would not Want the General Public to Learn that it is Possible to do as little as an Average of 2 Hours of Work per Day to Feed and Clothe yourself — that is, IF you are Set Up for Living, which Means that you would have to have a Good Fireproof Tornado-proof Hail-proof Paint-proof Termite-proof Mouse-proof Insurance-proof HOUSE, Home-craft Workshop, Well-made Tools, and a Luscious All-Mineral Organic Garden, Vineyard, and Orchard, which can be Obtained with less than 6 Years of Common Labor, without making a Slave of yourself, by Joining **"The Swanky Associations of Working Soldiers!" (A Fascinating Collection of Various Kinds of Voluntary Working Soldiers!)**, Book 018: beCause such Armies are Well-equipped for Mass-production of Beautiful Stone Dome Home Complexes, which have Marble-faced Walls, Granite-faced Floors, Skylights for Ventilation and Light, with those Luscious Gardens on the Roofs of all such Stone Domes, which are Water-proofed by the Installation of Ceramic Tiles. Indeed, a Swanky Stone Dome Home has Solid Walls that are no less than 10 feet THICK, which Stabilizes the Inside Temperatures, which can be Adjusted by Opening and Closing Windows and Doors at Appropriate Times, whereby all such Houses are Extremely Comfortable without Wasting any Money on Heating nor Cooling Bills, Chopping Wood, Burning Coal, Gas, Electric or whatever, which any Ignorant Rabbit would know all about; but, not most Americans, who are some of the most Proud Ignorant FOOLS who ever Lived! {See www.Amazon.com for: **"Are Americans the Most STUPID People who ever Lived?" (HOW Working People can PROSPER and Live in PEACE Under the Rulership of a RIGHTEOUS KING!)**, Book 047, plus: **"The LUSCIOUS All-Mineral Organic Method of Gardening!" (HOW to Grow DELICIOUS Satisfying Foods for Potential Kingz and Kweenz in Swanky PALACES!)**, Book 021, which is a Companion Book of: **"Orgimmick Gardening at its Best!" (HOW to Grow Delicious Satisfying Foods without a 10-Million-Dollar Investment!) By The Worldwide People's Revolution!®** Book 079.}

07-10 [_] O Adolf, WHO are YOU to be Criticizing Americans, seeing that it was the Germans who Caused World War 2, which was by Far the most Stupid War in History, which could have been Settled in a Courtroom, long before the War broke out: because Adolf Hitler BEGGED the Allies — namely, the British, French and American Leaders to Meet with him, and Work Out the

Problems in a Peaceful Rational Manner; but, the Allies were Rejecters of Truths, whereby they Refused to Meet with him, even as those Lying Edomites Refuse to Recognize YOU as a Force to Deal with: beCause you do not even have a Standing Army of Working Soldiers. ‡

— Chapter 08 —

HOW to get an Instant Army of Working Soldiers!

08-01 [_] There are presently some 2 Billion Unemployed or Underemployed Adults in this World of Woes, who would no doubt like to Earn GOOD Swanky Wages, which are First Class Quality Wages — such as 60 Dollars per Hour for Installing Polished Marble Tiles on a Stone Wall, at the Rate of 10 one-foot-square Tiles per Hour; or 50$ per Hour for Hoeing Weeds in a Garden, which will naturally be a Minimum Amount of Weeds: beCause **the Swanky Association of Professional All-Mineral Organic Gardeners** will have their Act Together, as the saying goes, and will thus have very few Weeds to Hoe: beCause of having them Under Control with the Correct Tools to Work with. After all, if you Hoe Weeds when they are little Baby Weeds, you can do it with the Greatest of Ease; but, when you allow Weeds to become Fully-grown, you are in BIG Trouble: beCause it might Require all of the Strength that you can Muster Up to get such a Weed Extracted from the Ground. Likewise, if you "Weed Out" any little Sins in your Life, and do not Allow them to Grow in the Garden of your Life, it is easy to Maintain a Clean Christian Life; but, if you give in to the Temptations of the Devil, it is equally as easy to get Addicted to Stinking Tobacco Products, Alcoholic Beverages, Drugs, Forbidden Foods, and whatever Capitalists have for Sale, who only Want your Money. ‡

08-02 [_] O Adolf, you seem to be a rather Religious Person, which most People are NOT, except with their Mouths; but, their Hearts are Far from those of the Gods, who only Do Good. Indeed, those Hypocrites might even Attend Church Services, and also Pretend to Read the Bible; but, it is all a Charade for most of them: because, in Order to Earn a so-called "Living" in such a Society as this, with its Great False Economy, one must Lie a little, Cheat a little, Steal a little, Rob a little, and do whatever is Necessary for getting some more Money: beCause almost no one is Set Up Properly for Living, as you have Suggested, whereby they might Live and Work at Home, in a Relaxed and Peaceful Manner, as People were Designed to Live, according to the *Bible,* which presents us with Adam and Eve in the Garden of Eden, who had no Bills to Pay, who were not Slaves of Edomite Bankers, Insurance Agents, and Tax Masters: because they were FREE with a Capital F. However, what are the Chances of us Persuading **"Seven Great Armies of Working Soldiers"** to get Up and go to WORK for 3 or 4 Hours per Day? ‡

08-03 [_] Well, my Friend, I would say that there are Good Chances of it: beCause of the Extreme State of Poverty that most People are now in. However, making Contact with those People is the Major Problem for me, since most People do not like to READ. Indeed, not one in a hundred like to Read Books, much less Good Books, which Bother their Consciences: beCause their Consciences are not Clean and Innocent, like those of little Children, who never Object to

Learning Truths, until they Sin, after which they are Ridden with GUILT, which can only be done away with when they Confess all such Sins, and Forsake them.

08-04 [_] O Adolf, why not just DRAFT all of the Young Men and Women into those **"Seven Great Armies of Working Soldiers!" (HOW to Provide a Way for Everyone to WORK: so as to Eliminate Poverty, Crimes, Drug Abuses, Prisons and Unnecessary Taxes!) By The Worldwide People's Revolution!®**, Book 015? After all, none of them will have to Kill anyone in any Hateful War; but, they will have to Build Up their Beautiful Muscles, and Learn HOW to Work Properly, Eat Properly, Sleep Properly, Clean their Houses Properly without any LIE-sol, nor any other Stinking Capitalist Abominations, and Dress themselves Properly: so that other People are not Lusting after them. In other words, they will have to Dress themselves Properly, as in MODESTLY, even as Jesus would do: because we do not want to make Whores of them. ‡

08-05 [_] Well, if another World War were to break out, none of the Nations would likely Resist that Plan, since they have Traditionally gone along with it; and some would be Happy to have something to Do, even if only to Murder some other Innocent Person, who was also Drafted into some other Hateful Army. Therefore, it would Prove to be an Interesting Experiment, since it has never been done, as far as I know — Thanks to those Lying Edomites, who are Dead Set Against any **"GLORIOUS Swanky Hotels Castles and Fortresses"**: beCause such Beautiful Planned City States would do Away with their Occupations and Countless books of Nonsense, which would be of no Interest to anyone: beCause, when you are Living in a Real Garden of Eden, of what Interest are Stocks and Bonds, Banker Scams, Insurance Scams, and all such EVIL Things? Therefore, if most of the Young People do not VOLUNTARILY Join those **Seven Great Armies of Working Soldiers**, we will be FORCED TO DRAFT THEM, whereby they will quickly Learn to LOVE it, and to Love each other. Indeed, they will just Naturally be Discovering Lovers and Marriage Partners, and especially if ALL of the Young Men and Women are Drafted, including the LGBT (Lesbian Gay Bisexual and Transgender) Community, who may also get Married and Live Happily there afterwards: beCause of Discovering other People of Like-mindedness and Similar Ambitions and Goals. After all, how many Young People have ever been Offered an Unlimited Amount of Money for doing whatever they might Imagine is Good for them, just as long as they have Good Plans to Follow? Indeed, they will be Welcome to Design and Build their own Beautiful Fortresses. †‡

08-06 [_] O Adolf, what makes you Imagine that it is EVIL to have Insurance and Health Care?
08-07 [_] Well, there should be Universal Health Care, which would begin with having LOTS of Fruit Trees — such as Mangos, Cherimoyas, Lychees, Yellow Sapotes, Avocados of certain Varieties, Peaches, Pears, Plums, Apricots, Apples, Cherries, Berries, Bananas, Papayas, and Low-acid Oranges, Grapefruits, Grapes, and especially Coconuts, Dates, Figs, and Japanese Persimmons, as well as all Kinds of Melons, Squashes, Kale Greens, Onions, Carrots, Tender Green Peas, and many Kinds of Vegetables, Grains, Beans, Seeds, and Nuts.

08-08 [_] O Adolf, I dare say that no one will have to be Drafted into any Army of Working Soldiers: beCause, just as soon as the Word gets Out that all such Voluntary Working Soldiers are Living in **"GLORIOUS Swanky Hotels Castles and Fortresses,"** all Sane-minded Young People will Jump onto the Band Wagon, so to speak, and go for it! Yes, they will be Happy to Earn those Good Swanky Wages, and say: "To Hell with going to School — I will get my

Education from Reading Good Books and doing some Practical and Necessary WORK with other Like-minded Voluntary Working Soldiers!" And therefore, no Draft will be Needed. †§‡ {See www.Amazon.com for: **"A List of FAIR Swanky Wages!" (The Equitable Wage System!) By The Worldwide People's Revolution!® Book 065.**}

08-09 [_] Well, X-amount of those Young People are Drug Addicts, who never did an Honest Day's Work during their entire Lives; and therefore, some of them might have to be Drafted, just to Straighten them Out, and Teach to them **"The Seven Basic Spiritual Building Blocks of LIFE!" (Faith Hope Trust Love Patience Persistence and Obedience!)** Book 036.

08-10 [_] O Adolf, I just HATE any Kind of Authority Figure Ruling Over ME! I Want my LIBERTY!

— Chapter 09 —

"Give to me LIBERTY, or Give to me DEATH!"

09-01 [_] The American Libertarian Political Party has that Saying as their Motto: beCause they Strongly Believe, and Sincerely Believe in LIBERTY, even while making themselves into Future Education Slaves, Work Slaves, Tax Slaves, Interest Slaves, Insurance Slaves, Drug Slaves, and Endless Bills Slaves of the EVIL Capitalist Empire, which they say is Based on FREE Enterprise and Christian Values! Yes, just Think about how GOOD that Word, "FREE," sounds in their Ears, whereby they Hope to have the Liberty to Rape the Earth of its Natural Resources for their own Personal Gain, without Realizing that the Good Old Earth has a LIMITED SUPPLY of Natural Resources, which should be Used WISELY for making all People Moderately RICH, and without Telling any Lies, nor Selling any Trash, whereby Capitalism has now Produced, Unwittingly, no less than 20 Trillion TONS of TRASH, much of which is Floating about in Oceans of Contaminated Waters! Indeed, it might even be MORE than 20 Trillion Tons, since much of it is Difficult to Calculate: beCause much of it is simply Dumped Out in the Woods and in National Forests and by the Shores of Rivers and Lakes. †‡

09-02 [_] O Adolf, along with Liberty, there must be Personal Responsibility as Good Citizens, which is something that a Person must be Taught in **"The Public School of IGNERUNT FQLZ,"** and in Churches, Mosques, Synagogues, Cathedrals, Temples, and in the Universal College of almost Worthless Nolij, which Wastes thousands of Precious Hours of our Tormented Lives with Pure Unadulterated NONSENSE! After all, what everyone in the World Desperately Needs, and Needs most of all, is Outlined in: **"HOW to Get our PRIORITIES in ORDER!" (The Glories of Democracy, and does Demon-ocracy have its Priorities in Order?) By The Worldwide People's Revolution!® Book 060.** Yes, if the Reverend Billy Graham had given that Special Sermon, about 60 Years Ago, Americans, Germans, and other Industrialized Nations, and especially China and Mexico, might not have Destroyed the whole Earth with their Capitalist TRASH, Junkyard Cars, Toxic Paints, Chemical Abominations, Radioactive Dung from ElecTRICK Power Plants, Polluting Jet Airplanes, and all Kinds of Stinking NOISY Toys, which People Lived Happily without for thousands of Years! †§‡

09-03 [_] Well, like most Americans, Dr. Billy Graham was also Greatly Deceived by the Bright Flashing Lights of Capitalism and Free Enterprise, which was Judged to be "Blessings from GOD," even supposedly from the Biblical Hebrew God, who Promised to Prosper those People who Believed in him and Obeyed him, which People never did Do since Ancient Times: beCause very few People Understood the WILL of God, much less Obey it. However, they did make a certain Zealous Religious Effort to do so in many Cases, whereby they Formed no less than 400 Major FALSE Religions with thousands of Contradictory Religious SECTS, whereby each one Claimed to be the ONE and ONLY True Religion — all of which have been DEBUNKED by our Selected King. {See www.Amazon.com for: **"Was Billy Graham Greatly Deceived?" (Giving Honor to whom Honor is Due!)**, Book 083, plus: **"LIGHTNING Versus the Lightning Bug!" (HOW almost Everyone can become Moderately RICH, without Telling Any Lies nor Selling Any Trash!)** Book 001, which is a Companion Book of: **"What is WRong with those Professing Christians??" (A Self-Examination of the Heart of the Body of Good Government!)**, Book 002, which is a Companion Book of: **"For the Love of Money!" (The Strange Things that People Say and Do to Get more Money!)**, Book 003, which is a Companion Book of: **"HOW to Prepare for CLIMATE CHANGES!" (The Wisest Plan for Mankind to Follow!)**, Book 004, which is a Companion Book of: **"WHY do I have to Surrounded by CRAZY PEOPLE?" (Do almost all People Feel like they are Surrounded by Crazy People??)**, Book 005, which is a Companion Book of: **"The Washington Journal is a FARCE!" (C-SPAN Managers are not very WISE!)**, Book 006, which is a Companion Book of: **"The PRAYERS of PUMPKINHEADS!" (Even God Needs a Little Humor to Cheer himself Up!)**, Book 007, which is a Companion Book of: **"A Sound Argument for Masters and Servants!" (WHY Everyone Needs a Good Master, and every Master Needs Good Obedient Servants!)**, Book 008, which is a Companion Book of: **"WHY are some Preachers so POOR?" (HOW almost all Preachers could get Moderately RICH without Preaching any Outlandish Lies!)**, Book 009, which is a Companion Book of: **"GOOD NEWS for REBEL WOMEN!" (HOW almost all Wives can become Moderately Rich without Leaving their Homes! GUARANTEED!)**, Book 010, which is a Companion Book of: **"The Low Court of Supreme Injustices is Brought to Trial!" (Our Elected King Butts Heads with the United States Supreme Court, with or without their Black Robes of Hypocrisies and Lies!)**, Book 011, which is a Companion Book of: **"The Right Design for Living!" (A List of Great Advantages for Building Beautiful Planned City States!)**, Book 012, which is a Companion Book of: **"The Gospel According to our Elected King!" (The Good News from the Most Modern Perspective!)**, Book 077, which is a Companion Book of: **"Poverty Hunger Riots Strikes Brutalities Election Deceptions and Civil Wars!" (The High Price that we Earthlings have Paid for Leaving the Good Land!)**, Book 014, which is a Companion Book of: **"Seven Great Armies of Working Soldiers!" (HOW to Provide a Way for Everyone to WORK: so as to Eliminate Poverty, Crimes, Drug Abuses, Prisons and Unnecessary Taxes!)**, Book 015, which is a Companion Book of: **"The CONSTITUTION for the New RIGHTEOUS One-World GovernMINT!" (HOW all Peoples can get True Justice, and Celebrate the Great Year of JUBILEE!)**, Book 016, which is a Companion Book of: **"The Great World TEMPLE of PEACE!" (The Glory of Jerusalem Arises Again!) By The Worldwide People's Revolution!®**, Book 017, which is a Companion Book of: **"The Swanky

(HOW to be Liberated from all Slavery, Worldwide!)

Associations of Working Soldiers!" (A Fascinating Collection of Various Kinds of Voluntary Working Soldiers!), Book 018, which is a Companion Book of: "GLORIOUS Swanky Hotels Castles and Fortresses!" (Beautiful Planned City States for WISE Intelligent Well-Educated People with Common Sense and Good Understanding!), Book 019, which is a Companion Book of: "Are you a Jobless Graduate of the SKQL uv FQLZ?" (HOW to get a GOUD EJUKAASHUN without Robbing the Bank!), Book 020, which is a Companion Book of: "The LUSCIOUS All-Mineral Organic Method of Gardening!" (HOW to Grow DELICIOUS Satisfying Foods for Potential Kingz and Kweenz in Swanky PALACES!), Book 021, which is a Companion Book of: "Did God or Satan Ordain Medical Doctors??" (Ask Huck Finn and/or Nigger Jim: because neither Tom Sawyer nor Judge Thatcher would Know!), Book 022, which is a Companion Book of: "The BIG White OUTHOUSE on the Not-so-Biblical Capitol DUNGHILL!" (The Chief Sins of the Divided States of United Lies!), Book 023, which is a Companion Book of: "The Public School of IGNERUNT FQLZ!" (HOW we have been GRAATLEE DISEEVD by Capitalism!), Book 024, which is a Companion Book of: "In thu Beeginingz uv Thingz!" (Thu Kreeaashun Stooree frum thu Beegining!), Book 025, which is a Companion Book of: "God Speaks and the Whole World Listens!" (Fire on the Mountain from the Burning Bush by the Spirit of Truth!), Book 026, which is a Companion Book of: "Does a Good Soldier have to be a MURDERER?" (Seven Great Swanky Armies of Voluntary Working Soldiers!), Book 027, which is a Companion Book of: "Thu Nq MAGNUFIID Verzhun uv Thu PROVERBZ uv KING SOLUMUN in Plaan Ingglish!" (The Understandable Version of the Famous Proverbs of King Solomon in Plain English!), Book 028, which is a Companion Book of: "UNLIMITED ENERJEE 99 Percent Pollutions Free!" (HOW to Obtain FREE ElecTRICKERY, Worldwide!), Book 029, which is a Companion Book of: " FREEDUM uv SPEECH!" (U Speshoul Maguzeen uv Onist Upinyunz!), Book 030-0001, which is a Companion Book of: "A Sure Cure for GUN VIOLENCE!" (HOW TO STOP GANG WARS and CRIMINAL SHOOTINGS!), Book 031, which is a Companion Book of: "AIIRMWVC and Reasonable Solutions!" (Aliens, Illegal Immigrants, Refugees, Migrant Workers and other Victims of Capitalism!), Book 032, which is a Companion Book of: "Mark Twain Races for the PRESIDENCY!" (The 2020 Presidential Candidates Desperately Need Some STRONG Undefeatable COMPETITION!), Book 033, which is a Companion Book of: "ECCLESIASTES UNCOVERED!" (The New MAGNIFIED Version of Ecclesiastes and the Song of Solomon in Plain English!), Book 034, which is a Companion Book of: "The Environmentalists' Paradise!" (HOW almost Everyone could be Living in a Beautiful Manmade Paradise!), Book 035, which is a Companion Book of: "The Seven Basic Spiritual Building Blocks of LIFE!" (Faith Hope Trust Love Patience Persistence and Obedience!), Book 036, which is a Companion Book of: "DIETS!" (A Reasonable Solution for the "Eternal Controversy"!), Book 037, which is a Companion Book of: "The Nature of CAPITALISM!" (A List of the EVILS of CAPITALISM!), Book 038, which is a Companion Book of: "SWANGKEENOMIKS Rules the Roost!" (HOW all People can Prosper in a RIIT WAA, and STOP Polluting the Earth with Capitalist TRASH!), Book 039, which is a Companion Book of: "The New MAGNIFIED Version of The Book of MORMON!" (The Story of the White and Dark Indians in the Americas!), Books 040A and 040B, which are Companion Books of: "The Great Worldwide TELEVISED Court HEARING!" (That Great Meeting of the Most Intelligent and Well-Educated Minds!), Book 041, which is a Companion Book of: "The Secret City of the Great King!" (HOW the True Church will

Escape from the Great Tribulation!), Book 042, which is a Companion Book of: "**Terrorists Beware that your Days are Numbered!**" (HOW to Bring those Terrorists Attacks to a Screeching HALT!), Book 043, which is a Companion Book of: "**The New MAGNIFIED Version of ISAIAH in Plain English!**" (The Understandable Version of the Book of Isaiah!), Book 044, which is a Companion Book of: "**HOW to Become a HOLY Man!**" (40 Good Reasons WHY People Should FAST and PRAY!), Book 045, which is a Companion Book of: "**The Proper RULES for FASTING!**" (The Complete Instruction Manual for True Repentance!), Book 046, which is a Companion Book of: "**Are Americans the Most STUPID People who ever Lived?**" (HOW Working People can PROSPER and Live in PEACE Under the Rulership of a RIGHTEOUS KING!), Book 047, which is a Companion Book of: "**An Amazing Collection of Wit and Wisdom!**" (The Marvelous Tale of the Colorful Peacock from Angel Ridge, and the Strong Rope of Everlasting Hope!), Book 048, which is a Companion Book of: "**Justifications for Capitalizations!**" (WHY our Elected King Defies the School of Fools by Capitalizing LOVE and HATE!) Book 049, which is a Companion Book of: "**The END of CONFUSION!**" (The Great CELEBRATION of the Magnificent Wedding of the Most Humble Honest Nations, and the Grand Year of JUBILEE!) By The Worldwide People's Revolution!® Book 050.}

09-04 [_] O Adolf, that looks like a TON of Reading! How in the World will Poor Innocent Johnny and Susan ever get around to Reading all of those Inspired Books, Carefully, with a Capital C? Moreover, if they did get around to Reading all of those Books, HOW would they be Able to Remember the Words of them?

09-05 [_] Well, that is where the GIFT of the Holy Spirit comes in Handy, which will bring all such Provable Truths back to our Memories, just as Jesus Christ Testified, which is HOW that I Remember all such Inspired Words, whereby I am Greatly Comforted by them. (See *John 14:26; 15:26, and 15:7*.)

09-06 [_] O Adolf, Junior, I will have to Confess that you are much more Spiritually-minded than your "Father," Adolf Hitler, who seldom Quoted anything from the *Bible*. Perhaps he never "red" it more than once or twice. Do you know whether or not he ever got into a Truth-brary?

09-07 [_] Well, my "Father" did not "wear his Religion on his Shirtsleeve," as they say, whereby everyone could Study it, Carefully; but, he had a very Good Memory, and therefore he only needed to read the *Bible* twice, in order to get the Basic Messages in his Head, whereby he could Meditate on those Messages, which gave to him a Great Advantage over most People, who have never "red" the *Bible* from Cover to Cover so much as one Time: beCause of Various Reasons and Sorry Excuses — such as, "It is such a BIG Book — I could never find Time to read it." Well, I have found Time to read it from Cover to Cover more than 20 Times, and have "red" parts of it hundreds of Times, which might Explain WHY that I have my own Versions of it. After all, it does lay down a Basic Foundation for Provable Truths, even if it is Full of Outlandish Lies: beCause those Lies are Like RUBBLE ROCKS in a Mountain that is Full of Gold, Silver, Diamonds, Rubies, Emeralds, Sapphires, Agates, Onyx, Marbles, Granites, and all Kinds of Precious Metals, Gemstones, and Deep Dark Sayings that one can Meditate on, both Day and Night, whereby one can Greatly Improve his or her own Mind, which most of the Children are Deprived of: beCause they are not Encouraged to Study all such Words, and

(HOW to be Liberated from all Slavery, Worldwide!)

Especially the Wonderful Words in: **"The New MAGNIFIED Version of The Book of MORMON,"** which most Professing Christians REJECT on Account of it being Associated with MORMONS, whom they Judge to be a CULT, which is all True: beCause a "Cult" is someone or some Group of People who have Beliefs that are Different from our own Beliefs, which Means that Jesus was a Cult Leader: beCause his Beliefs were the most Strange of all Doctrines in the *Bible,* which Caused the Scribes and Pharisees to Reject the Humble Man from Nazareth in Galilee, and Brand him a Son of Satan, when THEY were Actually of the Synagogue of Satan, itself, and they did not Realize it: beCause they were Blinded by their Great Pride: beCause of their much Learning, which is also what Spiritually Blinds the Minds of all High-ranking Professors, Teachers, Preachers, Politicians, Doctors, Lawyers, Judges, Chemists, Scientists, and Professional People on the Whole Earth — many of whom Judge me to be a NUT, even as they Misjudged my own "Father," whose Speeches are quite Rational, if you Study them Carefully, which I may Magnify, later on, if I find the Time to get around to it. ‡

09-08 [_] O Adolf, you just Revealed one of the most Profound Truths in all of the World, which I Doubt that most People Comprehended: beCause of being Spiritually Blinded by their Great Pride, which was also the Weakness of your own "Father," who was perhaps one of the most Proud FOOLS who ever Lived: beCause of his much Learning and Great Successes in the German War Game, whereby he nearly Conquered the whole World! Yes, it Required the entire Capitalist and Communist Worlds to Defeat him, as you pointed out before, which is very Interesting to Study: beCause, if the United States of America, for Example, set out to Conquer the World, even Today with all of its Military Power, it would be Quickly Defeated: beCause Russia, China, India, and many other Nations would GANG UP Against us, and easily Defeat us: because, Technically-speaking, we have no Great Advantages over them — such as your "Father" had over us and over the Communists, who Depended on Help from America, just to Defeat those Enthusiastic Germans, who Defeated Poland in less than one Month, and France within 6 Weeks, and actually had the entire British Army in their Control at one Time, and then let them go Home: beCause your "Father" was too Merciful for his own Good. Yes, he Believed that if he did GOOD for his "Enemies," their Hearts and Minds might be Won Over to his Side; but, behold, that Part of the *Bible* was Greatly Misunderstood by your "Father," who did not Actually Understand the Murderous Spirit of People like Sir Winston Cigar-chomping Whiskey-guzzling Churchill: beCause your "Father" was of a True Christian Nature, who BEGGED the Capitalists in Britain, France, and America to Confront him in a Peaceful Respectful Civilized Manner in a Worldwide Radio Broadcast, which could be Translated into all Major Languages, whereby the Masses of People could Judge for themselves concerning whomever they Believed was in the RIIT, and had the Best Master Plan for Solving our Problems. Indeed, Adolf Hitler was NOT the Murderous TYRANT and EVIL DICTATOR that Lying Edomites have made him out to be: beCause, in Reality, he was a Righteous Honest Person, who had GOD on his Side: beCause the Germans had been Greatly Mistreated by the Allies, whereby after World War one, the Allies laid a very Heavy Tax Burden on the Backs of the Germans, which Inspired them to Want to be LIBERATED from the TYRANNY of the Allies — from Britain, France, and America, whose Banks were and still are Controlled by Lying EDOMITES! Yes, they are at the Heart of the CRIMES in that Case. (Listen to the Enlightening Speech by *Benjamin Harrison Freedman,* an Honest White Jew, on YouTube Videos for the Proof of what I say.) ‡

09-09 [_] Well, my Friend, when the Gold of Truths is Refined in the Furnace of Afflictions, the SCUM will Rise to the Top, and thus be Revealed to all People who have Eyes to See. Trust me, **"The Great Worldwide TELEVISED Court HEARING,"** is the ONE and ONLY Reasonable Final Solution for putting those Lying Edomites in their Proper Places, behind Solid Stone Walls within those **"GLORIOUS Swanky Hotels Castles and Fortresses,"** where they can Manage themselves, Govern themselves, and Prove just how GOOD they are. Yes, that will Liberate them and us: beCause we will also SEPARATE ourselves from them, and Govern ourselves as we see Fit, whereby they will Lose their Dominion Over us. ‡

09-10 [_] O Adolf, you have not Addressed my Important Question. Indeed, I told you that I HATE any Authority Figures Ruling Over ME, which is still True: beCause I Want to be FREE! Yes, Give to me LIBERTY, or Give to me DEATH!

— Chapter 10 —

"Are we Tax Slaves of a Lower Order than those Lying EDOMITES?"

10-01 [_] Well, O Tax Slave, I also Love Liberty; but, only with Capital L's, as in LOVE TRUE LIBERTY, which is also Freedom from all Sins, Lies, Bad Habits, Evil Thoughts, Tax Slavery, Interest Slavery, Insurance Slavery, Sex Slavery, Debt Slavery, Work Slavery, and all other Kinds of SLAVERY, which none of you Libertarians have, much less the Dimwitcrats and Reprobates, who are the Promoters of all such Slavery, who Love those Hateful Wars, who Kiss the Asses of those Lying Red Jews, who are otherwise known as ZIONISTS, who have a Great HOPE of Ruling the World under their Dictatorship, which Calls for *"the Mark of the Beast,"* which we will Address in the next Chapter: beCause it is a Special Subject by itself. Indeed, it Implies TOTAL CONTROL over the Masses of People, which is a Lying Red Jew's Wonder Cure for our Ailments, both Political, Financial, Material, and Mental. After all, WHO could Fight Against such an EVIL Monetary System, once it got into Place?

10-02 [_] O Adolf, it seems like you were Promoting that Evil Monetary System in your other Uninspired Book, called: **"The Loathsome Burdens of the Independent Jackasses!" (A New Approach for Solving our Massive Problems!) By The Worldwide People's Revolution!®** Book 051. Yes, it seems like you Listed a lot of Great Advantages for Establishing the Mark of the Beast, yourself. Therefore, are you now Contradicting yourself?

10-03 [_] Well, I Believe that if you Study that Inspired Book, Carefully, you will Discover that it was someone else who Proposed the Use of that Mark of the Beast. Yes, it does have many Great Advantages over the Present Monetary System: beCause of Solving so many Massive Problems; but, it does not Offer True Liberty, nor Freedom from all Slavery, as I have Offered to you, whereby you can Work with Like-minded People to Build your own Beautiful Planned City

States, and thus Govern yourselves as you Please, with or without the Assistance of any Lying Edomites. After all, a RIGHTEOUS One-World GovernMINT has ZERO Use for any Banks and Bankers: beCause it Mints and Prints the Necessary New Money that is Needed for Building all such Beautiful Planned City States, which Stonework will Represent that New Money, which can have my Face on it, if you cannot Discover someone else who is more Worthy of it — such as Bernie Madoff, Janet Yellen of the Non-federal Non-reserve Edomite Banker's Scam, or the Resurrected J. Edgar Whomever, whose Top Secret Files no doubt contain some Important Information that would Prove to be very Interesting at: **"The Great Worldwide TELEVISED Court HEARING!" (See** Book 041.) Yes, perhaps you could put the Trustworthy Faces of Bill and Hillary Clinton on that New Money, along with Allan Greenspandex, Dick Chicanery, Donald Rummyfell, Condo Sleazy Rice Patty, and Obama been Osama; but, I would prefer a Seven-pointed STAR (✳✳✳✳✳), which would Represent the **"Seven Great Armies of Working Soldiers,"** who could possibly Discover the Face of a Holy Man to put on Future Coins and Paper Bills — that is, if **"The Swanky Association of Truth Seekers and Treasure Hunters, Worldwide,"** can Discover HOW to Produce MILLIONS of such Holy Faces: beCause of Discovering the Will of GOD, and **"HOW to Become a HOLY Man!" (40 Good Reasons WHY People Should FAST and PRAY!)**, Book 045. Indeed, it is for Sure than Janet Yellen did not Discover it, or else she might Persuade the Non-federal Non-reserve Bank (FED) to Publish all of our Selected King's Books, Worldwide, with the Assistance of her Honest White Jew Friends on Wall Street, who have all been Longing for the Happy Days when we are Erecting: **"The Great World TEMPLE of PEACE!" (The Glory of Jerusalem Arises Again!) By The Worldwide People's Revolution!®** Book 017. Yes, they have the Necessary Money for doing all of that: because they Control the Minting and Printing Machines, which they are Welcome to Surrender to **"The New RIGHTEOUS One-World Government,"** unless they would Prefer to spend the Remainder of their Lives in Slave Labor Camps, and Work in Rock Quarries, while Eating Insipid Rations of Recycled Sewage Water, Boiled Chemically-grown Tasteless Beans without Salt, plus Bitter Turnips, and Hot Green Onions: beCause their Usury Slaves have been Forced to Live on all such Things, and without any Mercy from Wall Street Chief Executives, who Eat those thousand-dollar Luxury Dinners with Rich People, and tell Dirty Jokes about the GOYIM, Huck Finn and Poor Nigger Jim, who do not have a Chance of getting into their High-ranking Class, nor would they Want to be in it: beCause they only Want to Live according to *Micah 6:8*, which reads as follows: {Please Check any Boxes with X Marks, if you Agree with the Statements.}

    A-[ ] *"He has shown you, O Man of Greater Faith, what is Good and Evil; and what does the Supreme Ruler your God Require of you, but to do Justly, and to Love Mercy and Forgiveness, and to Provide a Way for Honest Hardworking People to Prosper, and to Walk Humbly with your God: because you are in Charge of these People."* — NMV

    B-[ ] God has shown to you, O Wicked Man of Lesser Faith, what is Good and Evil; but, you have Willfully Chosen the Evil Way, even as all of those Lying Edomites have done, or else you would Deal Justly with the Masses of Poor People, and Execute Love and Mercy by Forgiving them of their Debts: because, who else on the whole Earth can more easily Afford to Forgive them, seeing that your Bank Vaults are Full of Silver and Gold, and your Stomachs are Full of Fat? Therefore, be Wise, and Humble yourselves, O you Edomite Bankers, and Provide a Way for all Honest Hardworking People to Prosper in a

Right Way: so that they can Live and Work at Home with their own Families, even as your God Intended for Mankind to do since the Beginning, and without making Slaves of anyone: beCause you have Mechanical Beasts for Slaves, and many Work Animals for Humble Obedient Servants, who will be Happy to Help you to Prosper, if you do not Mistreat them for the Sake of being Greedy Selfish Sons and Daughters of Satan, who is the Inventor of Capitalism, as well as that most Vile of all Institutions, called the Stock Market, which makes it Possible to Sell all Kinds of Abominations and Addictive Things. Therefore, Humble yourselves, O you Lying Edomite BASTARDS, before you Ascend into the Sky in a Radioactive Mushroom Cloud of DUST for your Just Reward, says the Supreme Ruler, your GOD! — NMV †‡

C-[_] I Confess that us Lying Edomites have Crossed the Line, and have taken Advantage of the People who were Born to be Servants, and have made them into our Education Slaves, Work Slaves, Tax Slaves, Interest Slaves, Insurance Slaves, Debt Slaves, Sex Slaves, and Endless Bills Slaves; but, rather than be Sentenced to Life in a NAZI Prison Camp for all such High Crimes in Low Places, we would rather Move into those **"GLORIOUS Swanky Hotels Castles and Fortresses,"** just for Cooperating with you, O Elected King! After all, we are not too Good to Work for a Living, nor are we Ashamed of our Inheritance. †§‡

D-[_] Damn your Souls if you Fail to make a Full Confession of all of your Sins, a Satisfactory Restitution for your Crimes, and a Restoration of the WHOLE Truth. †

E-[_] Educated People will Agree 100% that the Responsibility for Straightening Out this World of Woes lies at the Doorway of those Honest JEWS, who can now Willingly Choose to Hold **"The Great Worldwide TELEVISED Court HEARING,"** whereby this Madness can be brought to an END!

F-[_] I Fail to Understand HOW any Group of People could be Held Responsible for all of the Evils in this World of Woes, since we have all Contributed to those Evils?

G-[_] God Knows that, *"To whom much has been Given, much is Required."* — See Luke 12:35—53.

H-[_] I Honestly do not Understand all such Words.

I-[_] I Understand all such Words: because I am Innocent-minded. Moreover, I am not Attempting to Hide any Truths, nor to Cover up any Lies: because I am INNOCENT.

J-[_] Justice Demands that we Hold that Great Meeting of the Most Intelligent Minds, just to Discover the Whole Truth, whatever it might be, even if all TV Channels must be Shut Off, except for the ONE NBC TV Network that Publishes **"The Great Worldwide TELEVISED Court HEARING,"** which TV Networks are now in the Control of Lying Edomites, who can Repent and Cooperate, lest they all end up in those NAZI Prison Work Camps! †§‡

K-[_] King Jesus would not be so MEAN!

L-[_] Lots of Laughs! King Jesus would Fire Up those Crematory Ovens, himself, just for the Sake of True Justice — that is, UNLESS those Lying Edomites REPENT, in which Case, he would be Happy to Forgive them; and so should we. †§‡

M-[_] **"For the Love of MONEY"** they will not make their Confessions; but, we can Boil the Worst of them in HOT Used Motor Oil, in Saint Peter's Square, in front of the Basilica, and show it to all of the World, whereby they will come to make their Full Confessions, and thus Rid themselves of their Curses! †§‡ (See Book 003.)

N-[_] Not everyone will be Willing to Cooperate with you, O Selected King! Indeed, the Masses of People will Protest Against your TYRANNY, whereby you will FORCE us to Live in those **"GLORIOUS Swanky Hotels Castles and Fortresses,"** even in those Spacious **"Beautiful Swanky PALACES!" (A New Concept in Living Habits — Swanky Palaces for Poor People!) By The Worldwide People's Revolution!®** Book 066. Yes, they will REVOLT and take up Weapons Against you, O Unelected King: beCause they LOVE their Tarpaper Shanties, Mud Huts, Slums, Ghettos, and Swamps of Filthiness. Yes, they LOVE their Poverty and Squalor: beCause they were Born into it, and are thus Addicted to it, which can easily be Proven in a Courtroom! †§‡§§

P-[_] The Masses of People will Quickly come to their Riit Sensuz with the *Prodigal Son of Luke 15* when the LGBT Community goes to Work, and Voluntarily Builds one of those **"Beautiful Swanky PALACES"** for a Good Example — Thanks to the Assistance of that Multi-Trillionaire, our Selected King, whose Books have Sold more Copies than all other Books in the World, Combined — Thanks to the Provable Truths that can be Found in: **"The New MAGNIFIED Version of the Book of ACTS!" (The Understandable Version of the ACTS of the Apostles in Plain English!) By The Worldwide People's Revolution!®** Book 063! Yes, that is Possible, O Spiritual COWARDS, if we Sell them for him, and Promote them with Countless Advertisements on TV's and Radios: because of Seeing the Vision of Living in those **"Beautiful Swanky PALACES!" (A New Concept in Living Habits — Swanky Palaces for Poor People!) By The Worldwide People's Revolution!®**, Book 066, with Likeminded People, who have Patience, Persistence, and **"The PRAYERS of PUMPKINHEADS!" (Even God Needs a Little Humor to Cheer himself Up!) By The Worldwide People's Revolution!®** Book 007. †§‡

Q-[_] The Great Question is this: **"Will us Lying Edomites come to our Right Senses, before we are Stuffed into those Nazi Retorts, 4 or 5 at a Time, in Ovens that are Spacious enough to Accommodate us?"**

R-[_] This calls for a REVOLUTION, O you Nations of Education Slaves, Work Slaves, Tax Slaves, Insurance Slaves, Usury Slaves, and Endless Bills Slaves, whereby you can be LIBERATED by Means of **"The Swanky Sword of Divine Truths,"** and thus Move into those **"Beautiful Swanky PALACES,"** where you can Rest in Perfect PEACE with the Righteous People that you Choose to Live with, who Willingly Choose to be REBELS Against the Present Established EVIL Empire! Yes, all of the Brave Men who Agree with me should Wear Beards and Mustaches for Signs that they Agree to Rebel.

S-[_] Salvation is of the Supreme Ruler, and he alone can Deliver us from the Insanities of that Hateful Selected King, who Plans on making most of us Moderately RICH! †§‡§§

T-[_] You are Totally Insane, yourself! Indeed, the LORD has Revealed his Master Plan to our Selected King, whereby we can all be Saved from our MADNESS, whether or not it is Capitalist Madness, Communist Madness, Socialist Madness, Fascist Madness or some other MADNESS. But, first of all, we must be TESTED for our Worthiness to be Saved: beCause God has no Interest in Saving Ignorant FOOLS for Positions within his Holy Kingdom, who cannot even Understand such simple Books as this. ‡

U-[_] I Understand this Inspired Book, and so does my Mother; but, my Brother and Father do not Understand it, and even Refuse to Study it. Therefore, HOW are they going to be Saved for any Positions in the Kingdom of God?

V-[_] Various People will simply be Lost, and will never get to Live in those **"Beautiful Swanky PALACES"**: beCause of Rejecting Truths without any Justified Causes. Therefore, the Victory will be to him or her who Exercises his or her FAITH in ALL of the Provable Truths, and therefore Loves and Obeys them. Indeed, the Remainder of the People will be "Damned," which Means that they will not Obtain Positions in the Kingdom of God: beCause of not Passing their Tests of Faith, Hope, Trust, Love, Patience, Persistence and Obedience. However, if they only TRY to Do their Best to Love and Obey the Commandments of God, they may become Servants of those People who Pass their Tests, and thus get to Live in those **"Beautiful Swanky PALACES!" (A New Concept in Living Habits — Swanky Palaces for Poor People!) By The Worldwide People's Revolution!® Book 066**. In other Words, they are Righteous People for the most Part, who have certain Weaknesses that they have not yet Overcome, who will not Qualify to Govern other People during the Future; but, they may become Servants of those People who do Qualify, who will Help them to Live Righteous Lives. ‡

W-[_] Will we not have to Wage another Bloody Gory World War, just to Defeat those Lying Edomites?

X-[_] X-amount of Ignorant People might Imagine that such an Evil Thing will be Required; but, the Truth is Able to Defend itself in an Open Courtroom, where all Honest People are Welcome with their Cameras and Notebook Computers, who make Sure that they make Exact Quotations, which are not taken Out of Context with whatever is said, lest they should be Punished for it. Remember, *"It is a Fearful Thing to Fall into the Hands of the Living GOD!"* — Hebrews 10:31.

Y-[_] I would have never Believed it, just Yesterday; but, now I can Visualize Babylon coming to a Dead End.

Z-[_] The Zeal of our Elected King will bring it all about: because he has Yielded to the Will of God, who has put up with our Insanities for as long as he can Tolerate them. Therefore, if we Reject the Provable Truths that our Selected King Teaches, we will be Justly Rewarded with a Great Atomic Nightmare! Therefore, to Avoid it, let us Tax Slaves DEMAND **"The Great Worldwide TELEVISED Court HEARING,"** whereby we might Learn the WHOLE Truth, and nothing but the Truth: so Help us GOD! ‡

10-04 [_] O Selected King, I am now Wondering if it was God, himself, who Invented our Alphabet, or the Devil who did it: beCause it seems to be Prearranged to Fit Perfectly with every Statement that you make in all such Surveys! For Example, "A" Works Perfectly with Agree, while "Z" Works Perfectly with Zeal. Yes, it is Unbelievable how it could all be Inspired in such a Way, from A to Z, even as the Poetic Words of William Shakingspears were Inspired by some GOD, who Obviously Manages almost all of the Unique Writings of Inspired Authors; but, none on the Good Earth have ever been Greater than your own! †§‡

10-05 [_] So, are you saying that your Selected King is of a Higher Order than those Lying Edomites? Are you Confessing that your Selected King might have a Right to Govern us: beCause of being Qualified by his own Righteousness, while we are all Disqualified by our own Wickedness? ‡ {See: **"WHO QUALIFIES to Rule Over US?"** in a Wonderful Book, called: **"LIGHTNING STRIKES Versus Lightning Bugs!"** (HOW you can Become Moderately RICH, without Telling any Lies nor Selling any Trash!) By The Worldwide People's Revolution!® Book 074.}

10-06 [_] Well, being a Fictitious Character in a Fictitious Book, I have yet to Discover any Great Sins in you, O Adolf; but, as for that Selected King, I am not Sure that he is not another Sodomite, himself: because of writing about Greek Sex, as if it were a Good Thing. †§‡

10-07 [_] Well, being a Virgin, who has never had Sexual Intercourse with any Person on the Earth, during 70+ Years, I would say that our Selected King is likely the Best Man among us. Moreover, he is a Real Person with a Pseudonym, or Pen Name for "National Security's Sake," who would have long ago been Assassinated, if most People did not Vainly Imagine that he is Crazy, whereby they have left him alone. Indeed, not only have they left him alone to do his Writing; but, they have Encouraged him to keep on Writing: beCause of such Political Nonsense as one can Discover on C-SPAN, which Covers a Great Variety of Important Subjects, you must Confess. Yes, the *Washington Journal* begins the Day with a Multitude of Telephone Calls from Intelligent and Ignorant People, who Desperately Want to be HEARD; but, having such Disorganized Thoughts, very few of them make themselves Understood. Indeed, Representative Ron Paul, for Example, was put on the *Washington Journal* for the Sole Purpose of Demonstrating what it Means to be CONFUSED. Yes, he Sincerely Believes in LIBERTY with Justice for NONE: beCause, in spite of Tenaciously Clinging to his False Doctrines for many Years, and Consistently so, the American Parade to Hell goes right on: because neither Ron Paul nor Rand Paul, nor Speaker of the House Paul Ryan, have any Idea HOW to Discover the Doorway of Confession on their All-American Prison of Outlandish LIES — one of which Proclaims Liberty and Justice for ALL People, when, in Fact, there is no Liberty nor Justice for ANYONE! However, it all Sounds Good to a Spiritual Ear that is Full of the Wax of Unbelief, whose Possessor is Unwilling to Confess the True State of Affairs in **"The Divided States of United Lies!" (The so-called "United States of North America" in Disguise!)** Book 058. Indeed, it would be relatively easy for us to Demand and Conduct **"The Great Worldwide TELEVISED Court HEARING,"** as Opposed to carrying on with the same Old Sad Song for the next 100+ Years, and still not Discover the WHOLE Truth, whatever it might be, and all for the LACK of such a Televised Court Hearing, whereby the Masses of People might be Able to Contribute their True Nolij, and thus Solve the Problems. In Fact, only **"The Swanky Sword of Divine Truths"** can Win this Battle; but, only IF it can be Used Wisely in an Open Courtroom, where a Righteous Judge Presides, who is Persistent in getting the WHOLE Truth Exposed, even in all of its Stark Nakedness and Glorious Beauty, whereby we can all be Liberated by it, and take up our own Sharp Swords of Provable Truths, whereby we can easily Defeat the Devil and his Coconspirators, who are Determined to Flood the World with Outlandish Edomite LIES, which can easily be Proven to be Lies in a Righteous Courtroom. ‡

10-08 [_] O Adolf, if your Selected King is our God-Ordained Righteous KING, why does he not just say so, and thus take Over the whole World, just by Proclaiming himself to be that God-Ordained King? After all, **"The UGLY Scarred Dishonest Face of Poor Old Miserable UNCLE SAM!" (A Memorial Day Legacy!) By The Worldwide People's Revolution!®**, Book 054, is a Powerful and Persuasive Inspired Book, which should get the Attention of almost all People, Worldwide. †§‡

10-09 [_] Well, you might Think so; and even I once Thought so; but, most People are far too Distracted by their Toys, Games, Foolish Conversations, Tweeterings, and Televised Nonsense, if not by their Eating and Drinking and Using Drugs, whereby their Minds have been Warped Out of Shape, you might say, and thus it is Extremely Difficult to even make Contact with them in any Way.

10-10 [_] O Adolf, I Suggest that you Propose Branding them with *"the Mark of the BEAST,"* which might get their Attention!

— Chapter 11 —

The Mark of the BEAST is the Best Solution!

11-01 [_] When the Masses of People Refuse to Listen to Reason and Logic, it Calls for DRASTIC Measures — one of which is known as, *"The MARK of The BEAST,"* which is Detailed in *the Book of Revelation,* in the *Holy Bible,* which Predicts that an Evil Time will come when *"no man may buy nor sell without the mark of the beast, his number, or his name,"* according to Chapters 13—17, which often puts the Spooks into Unbelievers: because it Implies that there will be Total Control over them, whereby Liberty and Freedom will be Sacrificed to the Goddess of Injustices, which is the Chief American Goddess, who is not Worshipped by the Masses of People; but, only by the Governments of **"The Divided States of United Lies!"** Book 058. Yes, the BEAST is that Evil Empire that Imposes the MARK or NUMBER of the Beastly System on the Right Hand or Forehead of each Victim of Capitalism, who must Submit to the Will of that Evil Empire, or else Suffer the Consequences. Yes, *"the Smoke of their Torment Ascends Up forever and ever; and they have no Rest, neither Day nor Night, who Fail to Worship the Beast and the Image that Speaks Outlandish Lies."* †§‡

11-02 [_] O Adolf, *that* is NOT what the *Scriptures* Teach, and you know it for a Fact! Indeed, the People, who Cheerfully Accept the Mark of the Beast, will be Tormented both Day and Night — NOT the People who Reject it, as you have Suggested in the above Misquote. †§‡

(HOW to be Liberated from all Slavery, Worldwide!)

11-03 [_] Well, having more than 200 Mistranslations of it, I would have no Idea HOW you could Determine whether or not the Quotation is Correct or False. Indeed, I have no Idea WHY anyone would be Tormented both Day and Night for having a Social Security Number (SSN), whereby they might Collect Social Insecurity Payments when they Retire, which seems to be the most Compassionate Act which was ever Imposed on Americans in all of our History, except that the Payments are not half enough for anyone to Live on! Indeed, I have Proposed that all Retired People should have Swanky PALACES Built for them to Live in, Tax-free! Yes, those **"Seven Great Armies of Working Soldiers"** will be Happy to do that Work for them: beCause the Mechanical Slaves will be doing 90 to 95 percent of the Difficult Work. Moreover, many of those Retired People will still be Able and Willing to Hoe Weeds and Harvest Fruits for themselves to Eat, if their All-Mineral Organic Gardens are Set Up Properly. Yes, they will Rejoice just to be FREE at Last within their **"Beautiful Swanky PALACES,"** being Debt-free, also: because those Edomites will Freely Forgive them of all Debts, or else we will put them into those Nazi Ovens, and Roast them until they are Well Done, and then Feed them to Hungry Hogs, who LOVE Human Flesh! Just Kidding. Actually, we will Award them with Billion-dollar Bonus Checks for their Services. †§‡§§

11-04 [_] O Adolf, would you be so CRUEL as to Actually DO something like that, if you were in Charge of this World of Woes?

11-05 [_] Well, the Truth is that there will be no Need for it: beCause those Edomites will Gladly Submit to my Sharp Sword of Divine Truths: beCause, who would Want to Slave away for the Remainder of his or her Life in Rock Quarries, when he or she could simply Submit to the Sword of Truths, and Live in **"Beautiful Swanky PALACES!"**? After all, if those Rich Edomite Bankers cannot Afford to Forgive their Debtors, WHO CAN? Yes, they should Pray the Lord's Prayer, saying: *"Father, Please Forgive us of our Debts, even as we Forgive others of the Debts that they Owe to us,"* whereby they can be Liberated from their Bad Consciences; but, only IF they make Full Restitution for all of the EVILS that they have Inflicted on the Masses of People, which Means that they will have to Haul Out all of that Silver and Gold in their Bank Vaults, and give it up to the **"Seven Great Armies of Working Soldiers,"** who will use it Wisely for Decorating their Churches, Mosques, Synagogues, Temples, Cathedrals, Basilicas, Theaters, Concert Halls, Auditoriums, Gymnasiums, and Swanky PALACES, which will have Golden Thrones for Elected Kings and Queens to sit on! Yes, that Silver and Gold will no longer be Hidden from our View, along with the Warehouses full of Diamonds, which De Beers and Oppenheimer, Incorporated, will Gladly Sacrifice for the Sake of PEACE: beCause they have not Lost their Right Minds. Indeed, they might be Extremely Selfish and Greedy; but, they are not Totally Insane! After all, if they do not Willingly Submit to **"The Swanky Sword of Divine Truths,"** they will become Beggars, Eating from Dumpsters in Dark Alleys: beCause the Masses of People will Demand it of them, whereby DUMBmocracy will Finally SPEAK, and be HEARD! †§‡

11-06 [_] O Adolf, if everyone in the World is Issued a Personal Permanent Identification Number, similar to the Social Security Number: so that no one can Buy nor Sell anything without Using it in Computers, will those People not be Greatly Blest for it: because of getting Rid of such Problems as Illegal Drug Dealing, Illegal Immigration, Black Market Businesses, Tax Evasions, Child Support Evasions, Bouncing Checks, Counterfeit Money, Robberies for Cash, and all such Evil Things? Therefore, rather than it being a Curse, it will be a Blessing! †§‡

11-07 [_] Well, if you do not Object to Losing your Freedom to Sin with the *Prodigal Son of Luke 15,* I suppose that you could call it a Blessing. However, I Think that most People would Prefer to have their Freedom to Sin, just as long as it is not Hurting anyone else. For Example, the Alcoholic might want to get Drunk with Matt Dillon of Dodge City, "just for the Hell of it," whatever that Means; but, the Mark of the Beastly False Government would not Permit it: because it would Instantly Detect the Fact that such a Person is Buying too much Beer, Whiskey, Wine, or whatever. Therefore, such a Person would be Reported to the Government, who would then be Watched and Controlled by that Anti-Christ False Government. †§‡

11-08 [_] O Adolf, would you Permit some Wicked government to Brand *you* with any such Mark of the Beast? Would you allow them to Implant some RFID Chip under the Skin of *your* Right Hand or Forehead?

11-09 [_] NO! But, I would be Wise, and DEMAND **"The Great Worldwide TELEVISED Court HEARING,"** whereby we could Prove that no such Marks nor Numbers are Needed, except to Brand those Lying Edomites and their Lovers: beCause how else could we "Watch" them?

11-10 [_] O Adolf, I sure Hope to God that we can get the Masses of People INFORMED about **that Great Meeting of the Most Intelligent Minds**, before we get Branded with any Mark of the Beast: because the Masses of People do not Want it. In Fact, I do not know of anyone who Wants it. †

— Chapter 12 —

Freedom Comes at Last!

12-01 [_] Well, without a LOT of Cooperation from a LOT of Empathetic People, most People will never Hear about **"The Secret City of the Great King!" (HOW the True Church will Escape from the Great Tribulation!)**, Book 042, which is the Responsibility of whomever has Learned about it. Indeed, there is no Way on this Earth that one Poor Person can Advertise on behalf of all such Information; but, by "Word of Mouth," Computers, Tweets, E-mail Letters, Facebook Notes, etc., it is Possible that most everyone can Learn about it.

12-02 [_] O Adolf, if it is the Will of God, he will Provide a Way to Spread his Inspired Words, Worldwide, and in all Major Languages — that is, if it is of any Interest to him; and I cannot Understand WHY God would be at all Concerned for the Salvation of anyone, seeing that he Obviously Looks the other Way when Terrorists are doing their Evil Deeds. Otherwise, if he did Care, he could Surely STOP all such Acts of Violence. †§‡

12-03 [_] Well, it is not beCause God does not Care for our Welfare: beCause he does Care; but, it just so Happens that he has left us to Manage our own World, which Satan is in Charge of for the Time being: because God is Testing our Spirits for their Goodness. After all, he does not Want any Idiots in his Holy Kingdom; but, he does Want to Save all Souls from Eternal

(HOW to be Liberated from all Slavery, Worldwide!)

Sufferings, which is WHY he Sent such Spirits into this World of Wonders, whereby they might be Refined and Perfected for either Good or Evil, for Positions within his Holy Kingdom, or Positions within the Kingdom of Satan, the Devil, who will Eventually be put Out of Business: beCause his Work will be Completed, which is to Test our Spirits for their Goodness. Just Remember that God is Able to Raise us Up from the Dead by Causing our Spirits to be Born in New Bodies, which is otherwise known as Reincarnation, which is a Proven Fact of Life. In Fact, without the Act of Reincarnation, Jesus Christ could not have been Raised Up from the Dead: beCause "Reincarnation" Means, "A Re-entering of a Spirit into a Body." Therefore, his Spirit had to Re-enter into his Body, just to be Raised Up from the Dead, which is called the "Resurrection," which you could Doubt ever Happened; but, in a Courtroom, you would Lose the Case: beCause there is far too much Evidence to Confirm it to be True. For Example, would you allow someone to Crucify you, Boil you in Oil, or Stone you to Death for your Faith in some Fictitious Person, as in the Cases of the Apostles, who were Tortured for their Faith in Jesus Christ — at least according to the *Biblical* Account, which may be True or False? However, if the Stories are False, we would have to Confess that a LOT of People have been Greatly Deceived by all such Stories, whereby they have Believed a Pack of LIES! However, the Ironical Thing is the Fact that very few People have Believed and Obeyed the Teachings of Jesus Christ, which gives Credit to the Stories being True: beCause, if the Stories were not True, it is more likely that there would be only ONE Religion, and not thousands of them: beCause we have Modern Examples of such False Stories, which Produce Single Historical Beliefs, which almost everyone Believes in — such as Insanity Clauses, which come in Various Costumes; but, no one Denies that there is a Santa Claus: beCause he is just a Fictitious Character, which People Accept in general as being more Authentic than the Historical Jesus Christ, who left ZERO Evidence of his Existence, except for whatever is written in those Sacred "Gospels," or "Good Spells," which have Cast Deep Dark Spells on whomever Rejects the Provable Truths within them, which are still True, even if the Stories are Totally Fictitious! For Example, Jesus gave several Parables, which were made-up Stories of his own, which may or may not have been Based on Factual Happenings; but, that Part makes no Difference concerning the Truths within the Parables, themselves. For Example, if you Carefully Read the Story / Parable of the Prodigal Son in *Luke 15,* you Discover that you are also a Prodigal Son / Daughter, yourself, at least to some Degree, if you are not like the Brother of the Prodigal Son, who was the Better Person, you might say; but, he Lacked Empathy for his own Brother, who had simply been Deceived by Satan, whereby he Wandered in a Strange Land, and Wasted his Inheritance with Prostitutes, Drunkards, Gluttons, Gamblers, and whomever, which so-called "Friends" Forsook him: beCause the only Thing that they were Interested in was getting his Money: beCause they were False "Friends," even as most People in the World, Today, are Pretentious Friends, who often Present themselves with Grandiloquent Speeches, if they are Politicians, Professors, Preachers, and Sophisticated People; but, when it comes to Faithful Friendships, one might be Wiser to Trust Huck Finn and/or Nigger Jim: because the Tom Sawyers in this World of Woes are far too Foxy, and are out to get something for nothing, who do not much like to Work for a Living. Indeed, they are not known as the "Workhorses of the World," but as the Foxes, Coyotes, Wolves, Snakes, Skunks, Bears and Lions, who Prey on the Labors of others, which do not Describe the Character of Jesus Christ — Fictitious or not, which is hardly the Invention of some Lying Edomite, who would not even Understand HOW to Present such an Interesting Character as Jesus Christ, who is still a Great Puzzle to whomever Studies him, who was either the Chosen Son of God to be our Great King, or else he was the most Profound Liar who ever Lived! ‡

12-04 [_] O Adolf, has it never crossed your Weak Mind that those Lying Edomites had hundreds of Years to Perfect their Imaginary "Jesus Story," who set out to Invent such a Character for the Sole Purpose of Selling BOOKS, of which they have Sold BILLIONS! Yes, even *your* Uninspired Books Rely on that Fictitious Story for their Credibility. For Example, one of your Favorite Sayings is this: *"You shall Learn the Truth, and the Whole Truth shall make you Free when you Practice it."* But, you Ignore the Fact that no "Truth" can be Proven to be True: beCause there is no Evidence to Support it. For Example, the 9/11 Truthers say that Thermite was used to bring down the 3 World Trade Center Towers in New York City. However, no Thermite was Discovered by NIST (National Institute of Sciences and Technologies): beCause they did not Test the Scene of the Crime for any Thermite. Therefore, it is not True that Thermite was Used, nor can it be Proven in a Courtroom that it was Used at that Federal Government False Flag Operation. Therefore, the 9/11 Truthers do not have a Leg to Stand on. Likewise, whomever Believes that Government Officials Killed former President John Fitzgerald Kennedy is simply Deceived by the FACTS, which have been Presented in Various YouTube Videos and Countless Books. †§‡§§

12-05 [_] Well, you might not have Noticed it; but, I Noticed that you Proved yourself to be WRong: because the Negligence of NIST to Investigate and Discover Thermite at the Scene of the Crime did not Prove that Thermite was NOT Used; but, it did Prove that NIST was Negligent in their Duties, and Failed to be Scientific about their so-called "Thorough Investigation," which was a Sham, and a Cover-up for the Wicked Federal Government, which should be brought to Court for Failing to do their Duties, one of which is to Protect the Scenes of any such Crimes, until Thorough Investigations have been Conducted by several Different INDEPENDENT Investigators, including Civilian Investigators of Foreign Nations: beCause the Foxes, who were Hired to Guard the Chicken Houses, completely Failed to Do their Jobs, which was the Case for NIST, who were most Negligent of all: beCause it was their Scientific Duty to make a Thorough Investigation, which they freely Confess that they did NOT Do: beCause they were Covering Up for the LIES of George Warmonger Bush and Little Dick Chicanery, Incorporated, who were Obviously in on the Conspiracy that took place during September 11th, 2001, which could not have possibly been Conducted by some Bearded Gentleman in a Cave in Afghanistan, by the Name of Osama bin Laden: beCause only Magicians could have carried out such Phony Acts, and Osama was no Magician. For Example, when the so-called "Airplane" Crashed into a Field near Shank's Village, Pennsylvania, it left no Fire Burning, it left no Airplane Parts — not even the 6-ton Titanium Jet Engines, nor Wings, nor Cockpit, nor Fuselage, nor Seats — much less any Bodies, Blood, Guts, nor anything to Identify it as an Airplane Crash Site! However, the Vast Majority of Americans presently Sincerely Believe the Official Government Report, which is Based on LIES! So, why is that? Well, it is beCause they are "Pre-Programed" to Trust their Wicked Anti-Christ False Cover-up Federal Government, just by Repeatedly saying their "Pledge of Allegiance" to a Rag — Nazi Rag or not, which Spiritually Blinds their Minds, and makes them Vainly Imagine that it must be a GOOD Government: beCause the Vast Majority of the People are making such a Pledge, which Applies PEER PRESSURE on any Doubters and Sceptics; when it is Actually a BAD government with Greedy Selfish Motives in Favor of Rich Hogs called Edomites, even as Howard Zinn Proved in his book, called: **"A People's History of the United States,"** which should be Mandatory Reading in all Public Schools in America: because it Lists hundreds of EVILS that most Americans are not Aware of, nor do most of them Want to Learn anything about such Evils: beCause they Live in a Mythical World in their own

Minds, being like Naïve Children, who Accept whatever they are Told to Believe, and thus Pledge their Allegiance to their Rag — Nazi Rag or not. However, in the Case of the False Flag Events of September 11th, 2001, they made a Major Goof Up: beCause they Neglected to Conduct Honest Investigations of the Scenes of the Crimes, whereby they Incriminated themselves in my Courtroom! Yes, they might as well have Hanged themselves: beCause of their Neglect of Government DUTIES, one of which is to Defend the Nation against all Enemies, both Foreign and Domestic, which they did NOT Do. Indeed, the United States Air Force had the Official Obligation to DEFEND us against all such Attacks, and without any Special Permission from the VICE President Dick Chicanery, even as a Policeman has the Duty to Protect the School Children from any Terrorist Attacks without the Permission of the VICE President, or anyone else's Permission: because he is a Sworn Officer of the LAW, which does not state that any such Special Permission is Required. However, if you Doubt that little Fact, just walk up to some Policeman on the Street, and Dump Out your Trash Can in front of him, and see whether or not you get a Ticket, or perhaps get Arrested for it, and without any Permission from the Mayor of the City. Therefore, if a Policeman can Defend the Citizens of any given City, without any Special Permission from the Mayor, why could the United States Air Force not Defend the Pentagon by Force of Arms without any Special Permission from the VICE President? The Truth is Self-evident — it is their DUTY to Defend the People's Pentagon, as well as all other Domestic Structures in the United States, and even Ships in the Seas, if they are Able to Defend all such Possessions, which they were well Able to Do during September 11th, 2001: beCause they did Manage to Scramble and Deploy 2 Unarmed F-16 Fighter Planes toward Great Britain, that Fateful Morning, which Planes got Lost in the Confusion, and had to Turn Around and come back toward Washington — Thanks to Little Dick Chicanery, who got his Chain Links Discombobulated! Indeed, he Ordered them to "Stand Down," rather than Attack the Incoming "Enemy," which would have Saved American Tax Slaves Multiple Millions of Dollars, had the "Plane" or Guided Missile been Shot Down, as it should have been, and as it would have been, if President Eisenhower had been in Charge: because he was not Plotting any such Crimes with Osama bin Laden / CIA Executives; but, he was Aware that False Flag Operations were Possible: because Pearl Harbor was another similar Case, which was worked out by President Franklin Divinely-inspired Roosevelt, who Worked with the Japanese to make it Possible to get Americans Involved in World War 2, which put several hundred Billion Dollars into the Deep Pockets of the Edomite Bankers in New Yuck City, which can be Proven in a Courtroom, if anyone is Interested in it. Most People are not Interested: beCause, "It is all a Thing of the Past, which is now Irrelevant to our Present Problems," they say, whereby they Encourage every "Brainwashed" Flag-Worshiping Person to Believe that all such Evil Events should be Forgotten, when they should NOT be Forgotten, nor Forgiven, until Full Confessions are Made and Entered into the History Books, even as the Sins of King David and King Solomon were Entered into the *Holy Bible* by Honest Men, whereby Future Generations might Learn Good Lessons from all such Important Information, and thus not Repeat the same Vile Sins, which is the Whole Reason for having Courtrooms with Righteous Judges in Charge of them, with News Reporters Watching and Listening and Reporting the Whole Truth, whatever it might be. However, if you do not Object to some Lying Edomites making Eternal Education Slaves, Work Slaves, TAX SLAVES, Insurance Slaves, INTEREST SLAVES, and Endless Bills SLAVES of your Children and your Great Great GREAT Grandchildren for a thousand Years to Come, then why should I Care? However, it is now Possible for the Children to Discover what is being done to them in the Holy Names of Democracy, Freedom, Liberty, and Justice for ALL, whereby they might Decide to Abandon Ship! Yes, they might even Move to Mexico! After all, there are a lot more Freedoms in Mexico, than in **"The Divided States of United Lies!" (The so-called "United States of North America" in Disguise!)**, Book 058, which has a Tax Code that is some 70,000 Pages Long, when Compared with the Mexican Tax Code, which is only 7 pages long, and written in Words that almost everyone can Understand, while no one can Understand the American Tax Code, unless they are Tax Lawyers, which makes it almost Impossible for someone in the Divided States of United Lies to File his or her own Taxes without the Use of a Tax Lawyer, which no Poor Mexican could ever Afford, and would likely Help to Execute any Tax Collectors who might Attempt to Force him to Employ the "Services" of any such Tax Lawyers, when none are Needed, if the Tax Codes are SIMPLE, as they all should be and would be if Jesus Christ were in Charge — that is, IF he had any Taxes to Collect, which is Doubtful: because a Righteous GovernMINT has lots of Money to Work with, being Loved and Supported by almost all of the People, except for that SICK George Warmonger Bush CULT, and those HATEFUL Zionists, who cannot figure out HOW to Build their own **"GLORIOUS Swanky Hotels Castles and Fortresses,"** and also Generously and Cheerfully Help other Peoples to Build them, whereby they might all Live in Peace, and leave all other Peoples alone, and STOP making Slaves of them, and Murdering a certain Percentage of them. Indeed, our Selected King Explains HOW to Establish Peace throughout all Lands, and without Firing a single Shot, if anyone is Interested! †§‡ {See: **"The New RIGHTEOUS One-World Government!" (HOW to Establish a Righteous One-World Government without Going to WAR!) By The Worldwide People's Revolution!®**, Book 056, which is a Companion Book of: **"The Great World TEMPLE of PEACE!" (The Glory of Jerusalem Arises Again!) By The Worldwide People's Revolution!®**, Book 017, which is a Companion Book of: **"The CONSTITUTION for the New RIGHTEOUS One-World GuvernMINT!" (HOW all Peoples can Get True Justice, and Celebrate the Great Year of JUBILEE!)**, Book 016, which is a Companion Book of: **"The END of CONFUSION!" (The Great CELEBRATION of the Magnificent Wedding of the Most Humble Honest Nations, and the Grand Year of JUBILEE!) By The Worldwide People's Revolution!®** Book 050.}

12-06 [_] O Adolf, you are a very Long-winded WINDBAG, in my Honest Opinion, being Related with the Irreverent LOUDMOUTH Sloth-gut Windbag Hole-in-thy-Head! Do you not know that most People will be Turned Off by all such Windy Speeches, which they will call "RHETORICAL SPEECHES," as if it were a Sin to Use Reason and Logic to make a Point? †§‡ {FOOTNOTE: "Rhetoric" is pronounced "Redurik," not "Returik," nor "Retoorik," for some Strange Unexplained Reason. Therefore, I say that it should be pronounced "Ret-u-rik." Moreover, "Rhetorical" is pronounced "Retoorikoul," using a T, instead of D. See the KEE TQ PROONUNSEEAASHUN in: **"LIGHTNING STRIKES Versus Lightning Bugs!" (HOW you can Become Moderately RICH, without Telling any Lies nor Selling any Trash!) By The Worldwide People's Revolution!®** Book 074.}

12-07 [_] Well, I Confess that I do get "Carried Away," sometimes, as they say; but, I Seriously Doubt that anyone's Eyeballs or Ears were Hurt by it. In Fact, it might be Possible to Discover certain Faults in that little Speech, which can easily be Corrected during the Future: because that is what Computers are Good for; but, as for the Sins of this Wicked Federal Government, none of those Sins are easy to Repair, and Impossible to Repair without some Confessions.

12-08 [_] O Adolf, if a Skeptic can Discover so much as ONE Tiny Error within any of your Inspired Books, they will Use it for Justifications to CAST OUT all of them, while Mocking them forevermore: because you have Found Faults in **"The Divided States of United Lies!"** Therefore, you are not very Diplomatic, as a Good Leader should be, who should never Criticize his Readers nor Listeners, much less their Governments: because they all Worship their Rags, and Think of themselves as being Parts of the Greatest Nations on the Earth. Therefore, do not Criticize them, lest they should be Offended. Indeed, you have Deliberately Offended almost all Peoples on the Earth, for some Strange Reason that is not Understandable to me. So why are you so Insensitive to their Feelings? Are you a Narcissistic Megalomaniac, Pathological Liar with a Superiority Complex, or what?? How could you Profess to be a Christian? Would Jesus Christ run down **"The Divided States of United Lies"** by Criticizing it? †§‡

12-09 [_] Well, if you Imagine that I am Offensive within this Inspired Book, just wait until I get some POWER to Execute Justice for all Peoples, when they will call me a TYRANT and Radical Racist for Providing those **"Beautiful Swanky PALACES"** for all of the Poor People in this World of Woes: beCause those Lying Edomites Sincerely Believe that they are of a Higher Order of Superior People than the GOYIM (non-Jews), whom they Despise as being just a Grade of 2 above Hogs and Dogs, while they, themselves, are near unto Holy Angels! However, they need to Study: **"The UGLY Scarred Dishonest Face of Poor Old Miserable UNCLE SAM!" (A Memorial Day Legacy!) By The Worldwide People's Revolution!®**, Book 054, which Reveals the Truth about that Narcissistic Megalomaniac Society, which is Taught to be Selfish, Greedy, Proud, and Proud of it, which is also Extremely Hypocritical. For Example, they DEMAND that the North Koreans and Iranians GIVE UP all of their Nuclear Weapons, while the Americans and Israelis have Stockpiles of them in Warehouses, amounting to enough Explosives to Destroy the entire Earth a hundred Times over! And "Earth" is Meaning "the People of the Earth," even as it most often Means within the *Holy Bible,* which Refers to both the Land and the People, as if they were ONE and the same Thing, called the EARTH. Nevertheless, as True Christians, it is our God-given Duty to Point Out the Hypocrisies of our False Governments, even if it Offends a few Poisonous Snakes, Stinking Skunks, Barking Dogs, Grunting Hogs, Wily Foxes, Bloodhounds, Liars and Hypocritters. Indeed, we should Cast Out the Nuclear Trash from our own Backyards, before Attempting Cast Out the Nuclear Trash in other Nations' Backyards, and thus Lead the World by our Good Examples of True Christians.

12-10 [_] O Adolf, Junior, why did Adolf Hitler not Think of that, rather than Attempt to Exterminate the Jews, Gypsies, Palestinians, Iranians, and Homosexuals? †§‡

— Chapter 13 —

It is now High Time for Someone to be in Charge!

13-01 [_] O Adolf, most Capitalists have been left alone, to Govern themselves, which has Produced all of this Capitalist Trash, Pollution, Poverty, Crimes, Robberies, Thieves, Liars, Divorces, Murders, Broken Hearts, Arguments, Domestic Wars, Suicides, and all of the Evils that Follow after a Great False Economy, False Religions, False Governments, Injustices, Cruelties, Tortures, Prisons, Car Accidents, Plane Crashes, Terrorist Attacks, Medical Murders, Drug Abuses, Rapes, Teenage Pregnancies, Unwed Mothers, Fatherless Children, Gang Wars, Ugly Tattoos, Slave Labor Jobs, Recessions, Depressions, Obesity, Alcoholics, Drug Addicts, Mass Killings, School Shootings, Grade School Dropouts, Slums, Trashy Houses, Tornado Disasters, Hurricane Messes to Clean up, House Fires, Rotting Houses, Termite-eaten Houses, Rat-infested Houses, Cockroach-infested Houses, Bedbug-infested Houses, Mob Rulership, Mocked Democracy, Wasted Tax Money, Extravagant Military Expenses, Foreign Wars, Countless Refugees, Illegal Immigrations, Migrant Work Slaves, Extremely Rich Hogs, Starving People, Malnourished People, Sick People, Diseased People, Homeless People, Mentally and Physically Crippled People, Insane People, Expensive Rest Home Care, Greedy Funeral Home Services, Insipid Foods, Junk Foods, Poisonous Drinks, Recycled Sewage Water to Drink, Garbage Foods to Eat, Plastic Clothing to Wear, Noisy Stinking Vehicles, and you Name it — all for the Lack of Jesus Christ being in Charge of this World of Woes, who would lay down the LAW, and Enforce it with Submachine Guns, Bombs, Grenades, Mortars, Rockets, Guided Missiles, and whatever is Necessary to Correct us: beCause he is *"a Man of War,"* according to *Exodus 15:3,* which Saying has got to be an Invention of EDOMITES: beCause a God of LOVE would not be a Man of WAR! Indeed, "God" Means "All that is GOOD," and there is nothing Good about those Hateful Gory Wars, which Kill mostly Young Innocent Men, who may be PUFFED UP with Great PRIDE: beCause of being Taught Pride from Grade 1 and on; but, that is not their Faults; but, it is the Fault of those Ignorant People who Control them. †§‡§§

13-02 [_] Well, first of all, my Sarcastic Friend, you need to Examine your own Head: beCause it Sounds as if you have Lost your Right Mind (even though you have not), if you Sincerely Believe that Jesus Christ would Need, or even Want, any such Hateful Weapons, when it is a lot more Practical to Defeat the Enemies by Means of **"The Swanky Sword of Divine Truths,"** whereby People have to Submit to it: beCause they cannot Prove it to be WRong. For Example, let us say that little Johnny has been Discovered Stealing, should he be Sentenced to one Year in Prison, whereby he might Learn to become a Better Thief; or, should Jesus Strap his Buttocks with a Leather Belt, until he Promises to not Steal again?? Likewise, should Mexico drop an Atomic Bomb on Chicago for Mistreating Poor Mexicans, making Work Slaves of them with Extremely Low Wages; or, should they Present their Case to a Righteous Judge, who would Order Justice to be Done, or else have those Slave Masters made into the Work Slaves, themselves, just to get a Taste of HOW it Feels? Moreover, if someone cannot give up Stealing, all of their Possessions can be Stolen: so as to Teach to them what it Feels like. †§‡

(HOW to be Liberated from all Slavery, Worldwide!)

13-03 [_] So, O Adolf, what is to be Done for the Billions of People who are now Living in Slums and City Dumps — HOW will we Raise their Standards of Living without going to War, just to Obtain some Land for Building some **"GLORIOUS Swanky Hotels Castles and Fortresses,"** since most of the Land Belongs to RICH Hogs?

13-04 [_] Well, first of all, we will Kindly Ask them for their Cooperation, and Offer to Provide them with **"Beautiful Swanky PALACES!" (A New Concept in Living Habits — Swanky Palaces for Poor People!)**, Book 066, in Exchange for their almost Worthless Lands, which can be made a hundred Times more Productive by VERTICAL Farming within those **"GLORIOUS Swanky Hotels Castles and Fortresses,"** beCause of having all of the Roofs Covered with LUSCIOUS All-Mineral Organic Gardens, whereby no Land will be Wasted by Ugly Polluted Highways, Parking Lots, Shopping Mauls, Railroad Tracks, and so on: because the Electric Subway Trains and Elevators can Handle the Transportation Services, and 99% Pollution-free, which is Tolerable, when Compared with the Greatly Polluted Air, Water, and Land around present-day Cities of Confusion.

13-05 [_] So, O Adolf, if you were in Charge of the World, would you DEMAND that everyone should MOVE into a Swanky FORTRESS with Tall Solid Stone Walls around it, being like a PRISON, only a thousand Times more Livable? †§‡

13-06 [_] Absolutely NOT! But, I would Explain to the Masses of People all of the Great Advantages for Building all such **"GLORIOUS Swanky Hotels Castles and Fortress,"** and then Kindly Ask them for VOLUNTARY Working Soldiers, who might Want to Earn 60 Dollars per Hour for Setting Ceramic Tiles on Cistern Walls for Water Storage, since, just after AIR, nothing on this Earth is more Important than WATER, followed by SECURE Houses with Luscious All-Mineral Organic Gardens, whereby People can Feed themselves GOOD Satisfying Foods, without Chemical Poisons, Preservatives, and Capitalist Deceptions. {See: **"The LUSCIOUS All-Mineral Organic Method of Gardening!" (HOW to Grow DELICIOUS Satisfying Foods for Potential Kingz and Kweenz in Beautiful Swanky PALACES!)**, Book 021, which is a Companion Book of: **"Orgimmick Gardening at its Best!" (HOW to Grow Delicious Satisfying Foods without a 10-Million-Dollar Investment!) By The Worldwide People's Revolution!®** Book 079.}

13-07 [_] So, O Adolf, are you Assuming that X-amount of YOUNG People will simply Volunteer to Help Build such a City, and then MOVE INTO IT, get Married, and Settle Down like Sane People should? Are you not Aware that most People, and especially Young People are CRAZY!? Indeed, they Willingly Choose to Watch Murder Movies, and Play Violent Video Games, rather than Play with Fruits and Vegetables and Flowers in a Luscious Garden. †§‡

13-08 [_] Well, if those Drug Addicts get Hungry enough, they will just Naturally Consider going to Work within Swanky Fortresses, whereby they will soon Discover that it is not a Bad Lifestyle; but, it is in Fact a very GOOD Lifestyle: beCause, with my Plan, almost everyone in the World will Eventually become Moderately RICH, while Living in **"Beautiful Swanky PALACES!"** Therefore, just a few TV Programs about those Healthy Happy People within those **"GLORIOUS Swanky Hotels Castles and Fortresses,"** will ENTICE all Sane People to JOIN those **"Seven Great Armies of Working Soldiers!" (HOW to Provide a Way for**

Everyone to WORK: so as to Eliminate Poverty, Crimes, Drug Abuses, Prisons and Unnecessary Taxes!), Book 015, whereby they can all Obtain their own Swanky Palaces, according to their own Good Designs, which will Inspire many more of them: beCause the "Word" will soon get out that it is Possible to become Moderately RICH with only 4 Hours of Work on Average, per Day, 6 Days per Week, or the Equivalent thereof: because of using Mechanical Slaves WISELY for doing most of the Difficult Work! In Fact, if a Majority of the People are Wise, and Cheerfully Submitted to me, the DICTATOR, and Obeyed my Voice, it will not be many Years before almost everyone in the World will be Living in a Beautiful PARADISE, which will also be BOMB-PROOF and WAR-PROOF: beCause of the Good Designs of those Mighty Fortresses, which will be Impossible to Conquer from without, and Unlikely to be Conquered from within: beCause of Electing Righteous KINGS to Govern them, who have Filled Out and Filed on the Internet **"The Complete SURVEYS of our VALUES!" (SURVEYS of Religious Spiritual Political Governmental Sexual Social Moral Economic Business Labor Habitual and Miscellaneous VALUES!) By The Worldwide People's Revolution!®**, Book 059, for all of their Electors to Study before Electing them, who will just Naturally Choose the most Righteous Kings among them, even as they will also Study our Selected King's Surveys of his Values before Voting for him to Govern them from **"The Great World TEMPLE of PEACE!" (The Glory of Jerusalem Arises Again!) By The Worldwide People's Revolution!®** Book 019. {See www.Amazon.com for: **"Mark Twain Races for the PRESIDENCY!" (The 2020 Presidential Candidates Desperately Need Some STRONG Undefeatable COMPETITION!)**, Book 033, which is a Companion Book of: **"The Right Design for Living!" (A List of Great Advantages for Building Beautiful Planned City States!)**, Book 012, which is a Companion Book of: **"The Low Court of Supreme Injustices is Brought to Trial!" (Our Elected King Butts Heads with the United States Supreme Court, with or without their Black Robes of Hypocrisies and Lies!)**, Book 011, which is a Companion Book of: **"The Environmentalists' Paradise!" (HOW almost Everyone could be Living in a Beautiful Manmade Paradise!) By The Worldwide People's Revolution!®**, Book 035, which is a Companion Book of: **"The New MAGNIFIED Version of the Book of ACTS!" (The Understandable Version of the ACTS of the Apostles in Plain English!) By The Worldwide People's Revolution!®**, Book 063, which is a Companion Book of: **"God Speaks and Whole World Listens!" (Fire on the Mountain from the Burning Bush by the Spirit of Truth!)**, Book 026, which is a Companion Book of: **"An Amazing Collection of Wit and Wisdom!" (The Marvelous Tale of the Colorful Peacock from Angel Ridge, and the Strong Rope of Everlasting Hope!) By The Worldwide People's Revolution!®** Book 048.}

13-09 [_] So, O Adolf, it Sounds as if you are NOT a Tyrant of any Kind, at all; but, you are a Benevolent DICTATOR, who should be Loved and Obeyed by ALL of the Honest People, who would Build their own Swanky Fortresses, and Govern themselves According to their own Elected Laws and Flexible Rules, and thus Live in Peace with Like-minded People; while the Dishonest Deceivers, Liars, Hypocrites, and Ignorant FOOLS would Refuse to Join **"The Swanky Associations of Working Soldiers!" (A Fascinating Collection of Various Kinds of Voluntary Working Soldiers!) By The Worldwide People's Revolution!®** Book 018. And therefore, those Rebels will have to SUFFER with the *Prodigal Son of Luke 15*, until they Wake Up and come to their Right Senses, and Decide to Join one of those **"Seven Great Armies of Working Soldiers!"** Book 015. Therefore, Goodness will Eventually Overcome Evilness: beCause, more and more Righteous People will FORSAKE those Hateful Crime-infested Cities of Confusion, and Move themselves into those **"GLORIOUS Swanky Hotels Castles and Fortresses!" (Beautiful Planned City States for WISE Intelligent Well-Educated People with Common Sense and Good Understanding!) By The Worldwide People's Revolution!®** Book 019. Yes, it is an Ingenious Ideal, O Adolf! So, how come no one Thought of it, before NOW?

13-10 [_] Well, our Selected King Thought of it more than 40 Years Ago, in 1978; but, most People wrote him Off as being another NUT, just beCause of Dressing Differently than they Dressed! Yes, he has a BEARD, also, which Frightens them, if you can Believe it! {See the Cover Photo for: **"The Process of Making a RIGHTEOUS KING!" (A Fascinating Autobiography of our Selected King!) By The Worldwide People's Revolution!®** Book 082, which is a Companion Book of: **"All of the Arguments are in Favor of our Selected King, who has Zero Challengers!) By The Worldwide People's Revolution!®** Book 085.} Nevertheless, given enough TIME, and his Great Ideas will likely Catch On. Perhaps it is the Way that he Presented his Ideas, which Turned Off so many People? Perhaps it is only beCause most People did not get to Hear his Ideas, whereby they might Talk about those Ideas. And then their is the Greater Chance that they did not Understand his Master Plan, and even Vainly Imagined that the Federal Government should Print more of their almost Worthless Money for Hiring those Working Soldiers to do the Work, which would "cause great inflation," they say, which is TRUE: beCause it is a Great FALSE Economy, which is Organized and Controlled by the EDOMITES. However, that is NOT what he has Proposed!

— Chapter 14 —

Eternally Good Money without Inflation!

14-01 [_] I Mean that such Money is Eternally without any Inflation: beCause all of that Money must be EARNED by Honest Labor, without any Loans, without any Interest / Usury, and without any Taxes! For Example, One Hour of Common Labor will always be Worth One Hour of Common Labor. Therefore, if you are an Extra Smart Gardener, and get your Act Together, as they say, you will be able to do 30 Minutes or less of Work in your Garden per Day, on Average, and have an Abundance of Foods to Eat, if you Preserve them in your Walk-in Cooler / Root Cellar or Freezer. For Example, you will be able to Harvest your Apples at the Peak of Perfection, and Store them in your Walk-in Cooler, which will be at least 30 feet in Diameter, being Square (surrounding a Walk-in Freezer / Ice House that is 12 feet in Diameter on the Inside), having Concrete Shelves a foot apart, going all around the Walk-in Cooler Room, being Faced with Ceramic Tiles on all Shelves, Walls, and Floors, whereby you will easily be able to Clean the entire Room with Hot Water under Pressure, which will Drain into the Garden: so that no Water is Wasted; and the Garden will Drain into a Cistern, after the Water has been Filtered and Purified, Naturally. Indeed, our Selected King has Explained it in great Details in: **"The LUSCIOUS All-Mineral Organic Method of Gardening!" (HOW to Grow DELICIOUS Satisfying Foods for Potential Kingz and Kweenz in Beautiful Swanky PALACES!)**, Book 021, which is a Companion Book of: **"Orgimmick Gardening at its Best!" (HOW to Grow Delicious Satisfying Foods without a 10-Million-Dollar Investment!) By The Worldwide People's Revolution!®**, Book 079, which contains many Colorful Photographs with Enlightening Explanations. Therefore, if the Garden and Cooler are set up Properly, along with a Spacious Canning Kitchen, any Family, or even a Single Person, can do as little as 2 Months of Common Labor per Year, and Eat like Royalties — Thanks to **"The Swanky Association of Professional Organic Gardeners,"** and **"The Swanky Association of Professional Cooks,"** which will Assist everyone to get Set Up Properly with Canning Jars and Tools, which will be Produced by **"The Swanky Association of Tool Makers,"** who will Work Together with many other Associations of Working Soldiers, who will Volunteer to do 4 Hours of Common Labor per Day, 6 Days per Week, or the Equivalent thereof, and have the remainder of the Day for themselves, to do their own Gardening, House Cleaning, Work in their Home-craft Workshop, or go Sightseeing! Indeed, they will be Free to do whatever they Want to do, and also Vote for whatever Gardening Plan that they Like Best, which might include Community Gardens, as well as Private Home Gardens. Indeed, some Old People might only Want Small Vegetable Gardens and Flower Gardens: beCause of taking the Electric Elevators and Subway Trains to **Royal Swanky Buffets**, where they can Eat all that they might Want for FREE! ‡

14-02 [_] So, O Adolf, if we Preferred to NOT Work in our own Gardens, would **"The Swanky Association of Professional Organic Gardeners"** do the Work to Grow all of our Foods, and take Care of them Properly? For Example, I would much rather spend my Time making Fine Hand-crafted Furniture, than Hoeing Weeds in a Garden.

14-03 [_] Well, whatever makes you Healthy and Happy is most Important; and almost nothing on this Earth makes People as Healthy nor as Happy as Organic Gardening, if they Eat the Foods that they Grow, which they will be Happy to Do, IF those Foods Taste Extra Special, which they will, if they are Grown Properly, having the Necessary Minerals in the Topsoil, which is a SCIENCE, and not just a Thing of CHANCE, as it now is with most Gardeners, who have no Idea how GOOD all such Foods can Taste, if they have the Right Topsoil, the Right Seeds, the Right Amount of Water, and the Right Amount of Natural Fertilizers, which not even the Queen of England presently has: beCause of a Lack of the Proper Amount of Sunlight! Yes, England is very Good for Growing Green Grasses, Grazing Sheeps and Cattle, and Fox Hunting; but, when it comes to Growing very Sweet Tasty Fruits, there is not enough Sunlight for it, with the Exception of Various Kinds of Berries, which Tolerate Shade. Therefore, they might have to Eat mostly Imported Foods, if they Want really Tasty Fruits and Vegetables, which is no Problem: because they can Trade Mutton for it, and Grow Various Kinds of Nuts: because Nut Trees can also Tolerate more Shade and Foggy Weather than Fruit Trees, which are prone to Contract Diseases: beCause of the Dampness of the Weather. Certain Vegetables also do not Object to Damp Weather — such as Kale Greens and Collards. Therefore, when People are Living in such Conditions, they have to Learn to be Flexible. Personally, I would Move to a Better Climate, where there is Plenty of Sunlight for the Fruit Trees, and the Ground is not "Washed Out" by too much Rain, as it might be in Seattle, Washington. †‡

14-04 [_] So, O Adolf, if there is no Money Loaned to anyone: beCause of not having any Bankers, all Money will have to be Earned by Honest Labor for the Construction of those Beautiful Planned City States; and therefore, it will be Impossible to have any INFLATION on that Money: beCause the Economy will not be Flooded with an Excessive Amount of Money at any Time: beCause People can only do so much Work to Earn such Money, which they could Earn more of, if they should Work for 8 to 12 Hours per Day; but, there is no Need for it: beCause all of the Building Materials will be FREE for those Working Soldiers to Work with, if you are in Charge of everything — RIIT?

14-05 [_] Yes, that is Correct — it will be Impossible to have any Inflation on the Money, whereby it might be "Devalued" by Printing and Spending too much of it. However, I Recommend that everyone should Save as much of their Money as Possible, just in Case they Decide to BUY certain Portions of their Stone Dome Home Complexes — such as their Workshops and Sales Shops, whereby they can Modify them in any Way that they Like. For Example, someone might not like the Colorful Ceramic Tiles on the Kitchen Walls, and Want to Replace them with White Marble, without Understanding that Marble is POROUS, which Means that it can Absorb Oils, Grease, and Juices that might Stain it, while Ceramic Tiles are Impermeable, being like Glass and Chinaware, which is much Better for a Kitchen. However, if such a Person wants to Buy the Kitchen, he or she may do whatever he or she Pleases with it: beCause it is his or her Property. After all, **"The Swanky Association of Professional Designers"** will do their Best to make every Room in every House as Beautiful and Attractive as Possible, after going to School to Learn HOW. Therefore, if you are such an Artistic Person with Great Designs in your Head for all such Beautiful Things, you should Join that Association, and Contribute your Talents. After all, that will be one of the Primary Occupations for all such Construction Projects: beCause every Fortress and every Room should be UNIQUE and Special, which is made Possible by PAINTS on Colored Ceramic Tiles. Indeed, you could Paint Beautiful

Murals for Ceramic-faced Walls, if you are an Artist. Therefore, Artists will get their Day of Justice with Good Swanky Wages, if they are Good at it; and the Best of them will be Invited to Design Special Swanky Castles and Hotels! ‡

{FOOTNOTE: The above Photo is in Black and White; but, that is to Save you some Money on the Cost of the Book. However, if you Want to See a Colored Picture of it, you should Check Out Page 49, called: **"LIGHTNING STRIKES Versus Lightning Bugs!" (HOW you can Become Moderately RICH, without Telling any Lies nor Selling any Trash!) By The Worldwide People's Revolution!®** Book 074. You can also see Close-up Views in other Books. Moreover, you could use any Colors of Ceramic Tiles that you might Like for making your own **"Beautiful Swanky PALACES!" (A New Concept in Living Habits — Swanky Palaces for Poor People!)**, Book 066, which could have Unique False Faces on THICK Stone Walls, which are Designed for FREE Heating and Cooling, much like the Pantheon in Rome, which you can see a Photo of on Page 40 of Book 074. Use your Imagination, seeing that you were somewhat Created in the Image of God, who has a Great Imagination! But, if you Doubt it, just Check Out the many YouTube Videos about Animals, beginning with the Birds and Fishes. Try Searching for: "Top 10 Most Beautiful Birds in the World," followed by: "The World's Strangest Fruits," "Dubai Miracle Gardens," and "The Most Beautiful Gardens in Europe," and Plan on taking a Week to do it: beCause it will not be a Waste of your Precious Time. And do not Forget to Finish Reading this Inspired Book for more Inspiration after being Distracted by all of those Good Things.}

14-06 [_] O Adolf, your "Father" was an Artist, in Austria, whose Paintings were not Greatly Appreciated at that Time, even though he was very Good at it. Therefore, will all such Paintings be Imposed on Ceramic Tiles of Various Sizes, whereby they can be Preserved?

14-07 [_] Well, I Recommend it, even for the Pornographers, who can Paint or Print their Nude Subjects on large Ceramic Tiles, and Install them on the Walls of a Nudist Colony, just for their Pleasure and Entertainment, whereby they can finally get Satisfied by having Millions of Naked People all over their Walls, even as the Ancient Greeks had them all over their Ceramic Vases, which Decorated their Houses. Yes, most of the Wealthier Houses had Statues of Nude Young Men: beCause they had a Great Appreciation for Beautiful Human Bodies: beCause of considering the Fact that such Bodies are the Crowning Work of the Great Creator God, when they are in Good Health. Therefore, many Young People will no doubt be "Immortalized" on large Ceramic Tiles in all such Fortresses. ‡ {See www.Man2ManAlliance.org for Documented Evidence of the Ancient Greeks, who did not Suffer with Rapes, Murders, Infidelities, nor any of the American Sexual Sins, Unwed Mothers, Fatherless Children, nor any such Evil Things.}

14-08 [_] O Adolf, are you not at all Concerned that such Fortresses will become Extremely Corrupted by Horny Old Men, who will be Preying on all such Beautiful Young Men, and perhaps Raping them: beCause of being Over-stimulated by BAD Diets?

14-09 [_] Well, that is WHY it is very Important for everyone to Fill Out and FILE **"The Complete Surveys of our VALUES,"** Book 059, whereby all such People can be "Screened Out," and thus all of those Wise People can Live in Peace. Nevertheless, whatever the Case, it will Prove to be an Interesting Experiment, which everyone will be Able to Learn Good Lessons from, and thus come to Rational Conclusions about making Paintings, Pictures and Statues of Nude People. Personally, I would much Prefer to have just one Healthy Happy Lover, and Practice Fidelity, and have NO Paintings nor Pictures on the Walls of Naked People, even as Beautiful as they are: beCause it is Over-stimulating to a Person's Mind, and especially to a Young Mind, which might Cause such a Young Person to Want such Flesh to Lust after, without considering the Consequences of Fornication in a Whorehouse, whereby it is Demeaning, Degrading, Degenerating, Depressing, and Dangerous: beCause there are hundreds of Sexually-transmitted Diseases, which can also Prove to be Fatal, if not Treated Properly by much Fasting and Praying and Eating Correctly from there onward. Indeed, I would rather Avoid all such Evils; but, you are Welcome to Do whatever you Decide is Best for you. ‡

14-10 [_] O Adolf, what if some Bully takes Over a Swanky Fortress from within it, and begins to Order everyone about, like some Tyrant King — HOW will we get Rid of him? For Example, Donald Trumpeter seems to be a Big BULLY, who Orders Protestors to LEAVE his Meetings, when he should Respectfully Answer their Questions, and Present himself as a Presidential Person, instead of a Big BULLY, which is Disgusting, at least to me. However, some People Like Bullies: because they seem to be in Command of Things, whereby they Appear to be Leaders; but, not in my Viewpoint.

— Chapter 15 —

Bullies will not be in Charge!

15-01 [_] Well, when a Person has **"The Swanky Sword of Divine Truths"** on his Side of every Issue, there is no Need for Acting like a Bully: beCause the Truth will easily Defeat any Enemy, if that Truth is Presented to the Masses of People in its Wholeness, Purity, and with Reason and Logic. Indeed, the Truth only Asks for a Fair Hearing. For Example, Americans in general might Argue that their Wooden / Plastic Firetrap Houses are GOOD, and even "Beautiful." However, the Masses of People in the whole World would Disagree with them, after Learning the FACTS about all such Houses — such as the Fact that they Require Constant Repairs, Replacements of Carpets, Fire Insurance, and Spraying for Termites — not to Mention Frozen Water Pipes, Heating and Cooling Bills, Paint Jobs, Broken Windows fixed, Ruined Screen Doors Replaced with similar Trash, Hedges Trimmed and Lawns Mowed, which Expenses amount to thousands of dollars per Year, and the ever-present Danger of being Blown Away by Tornadoes! Yes, tens of thousands of such almost Worthless Houses are Destroyed by one Means or another, Annually: beCause they are Designed by Satan and Sons, Incorporated! Therefore, the Masses of People in this World would just Naturally Agree with me that there are Vast Spaces for Improvements on American Houses. Indeed, who could Argue that Polished Marble Walls need to be PAINTED? ‡

15-02 [_] O Adolf, People might get Tired of Looking at those UGLY Marble Walls; and therefore, they might Want to Paint their Walls. Therefore, as a BIG Bully, would you DEMAND that everyone should have Polished Marble Walls, Granite-faced Walls, Ceramic-faced Solid Stone Walls, or Concrete Walls with Tiles, as Opposed to having Beautiful PAINTS on Wooden-plasterboard Walls, or Sheetrock Walls?

15-03 [_] NO! I would not Demand any such Things: beCause everyone must have their Freedom to Choose what they Want, even if they Want to Live in **"The BIG White OUTHOUSE on the Not-so-Biblical Capitol DUNGHILL!"** Book 023. However, I would say that if anyone Prefers UGLY Painted Walls, after Visiting the *Shrine of Immaculate Conceptions for Holy Virgins,* in Washington, D.C., or *the Palace of Beautiful Arts* in Mexico City, or *Saint Peter's Basilica* in Rome, or even my own "Palace," such a Person should have his or her Head Examined for some "Loose Screws": because he or she is Obviously INSANE! †§‡

15-04 [_] O Adolf, I would say that whomever did not Check Box 15-03 should not be Permitted to Live in those **"GLORIOUS Swanky Hotels Castles and Fortresses"**: beCause they are Mentally SICK, being Religious NUTS: beCause the New Jerusalem that is coming down from Heaven is a Marvelous Mansion with many Marble, Onyx, and Granite Houses, which are far more Beautiful than anything on the Earth! Indeed, there would not be any Ugly Paint found in the whole City, nor any other Abominations, including those Stinking Noisy Vehicles, Lawnmowers, Weed-eaters, Snow Blowers, Leaf Blowers, Motorcycles, Motor Scooters, nor even Bicycles: because People will Travel by the Power of the Spirit of God! See *Revelation 21, Gay King James Version (KJV).* †§‡

15-05 [_] Well, I would say that whomever does not Agree to Help Build those **"GLORIOUS Swanky Hotels Castles and Fortresses,"** is a Potential Enemy / Terrorist / Anti-Christ, Dawter of Satan, Rapist, Thief, Robber, Murderer, Adulterer, Greedy Selfish Son of Satan, or whatever, who should have to Live in some City of Confusion with other Criminals, until they Wake Up and come to their Right Senses with the *Prodigal Son of Luke 15,* who Changed his Mind, and Decided to go back Home to his Father, and Confess his Sins. Indeed, after making Education Slaves, Work Slaves, Tax Slaves, Interest Slaves, Insurance Slaves, Sex Slaves, Debt Slaves, and Endless Bills Slaves of themselves for Decades, one would Think that they would be SICK of it! But, if they are not Sick of it, let them Suffer with more and more of it, until they come to their Right Senses. Otherwise, Try to Enlighten their Minds by Offering a Copy of this Book to them.

15-06 [_] O Adolf, just as long as People's Stomachs are Full of Foods, they will never come to their Right Senses: beCause the Brains do not Function Correctly under such Evil Conditions. Otherwise, almost everyone in the whole World would Agree with you. Moreover, as long as they are Addicted to Drugs, Alcohol, Junk Foods, Automobiles, Televisions, and all such Evil Things, there is no Hope for them to Accept the TRUTHS that you and your Selected King Teach: beCause their Minds are Spiritually Blinded. Therefore, it is a Hopeless Cause. †§‡

15-07 [_] Well, I Naturally Reject that Notion — that it is a Hopeless Cause: beCause People Change their Minds all of the Time, which follows the "Hundredth Monkey Theory," whereby the Masses of People finally "Catch On," after X-amount of other Monkeys "Catch On," who are the more Intelligent "Monkeys," who can be the Elite Class, the Middle Class, the Low Class, or just any Intelligent Group of Smarter People, who Recognize a Good Thing when they Learn about it — such as the 5,000+ Good Reasons and Great Advantages for Building Beautiful Planned City States, whereby Terrorists are "Sterilized or Castrated" by **"The Swanky Sword of Divine Truths,"** and thus made Impotent! Indeed, ISIS (Israeli Secret Instigation Services) would not be Able to Do its Evil Deeds in the Middle East, if the Masses of People over there began to Build those **"GLORIOUS Swanky Hotels Castles and Fortresses"**: beCause, Like-minded People would be Working on the Construction of them, and would be Protected by **"The New RIGHTEOUS One-World Government,"** which the Masses of People in this World of Woes would Gladly Join: beCause of the Potential of becoming Moderately Rich, just by their Labors, alone, without Borrowing any Money, without going into Debt, and without being Taxed for Building **"Beautiful Swanky PALACES"** for themselves! Yes, it is all Explained in Great Details within Good Books, if anyone is Interested in Learning about all such Things. (See Verse 09-03.)

15-08 [_] O Adolf, only a Small Percentage of the Masses of People like to READ Books, and only a Small Percentage of those People like to read such Uninspired Books as you write, which are Extremely BORING, which make most People SICK, just to read a Sentence or 2: beCause of all of the Capitalized Words, which have no **"Justifications for Capitalizations!"** (Book 049.) Indeed, they just Naturally Conclude that you are a NUT — a CRAZY Person, who should go to some Elementary Grade School and Learn HOW to Write Properly: beCause "LOVE," for Example, should never be Capitalized with a large L, except in the Titles of Books and Newspaper Articles: beCause the *"Love of God,"* for Example, is not nearly as Important as the *"Love of Money,"* which makes it Possible for us to Prosper with True Prosperity, whereby almost everyone in China, for Example, is Choking on their own Pollution: beCause of Mass-producing all Kinds of Capitalist JUNK, which no one ever Needed for True Prosperity. †§‡§§ {See www.Amazon.com for: **"The Great False Economy is now DEBUNKED!" (Adolf Hitler had a much Better Economic System!) By The Leader, Adolf Dictator Hitler, Junior!** Book 053.}

15-09 [_] Well, if my Inspired Books are so BORING, why are you Reading them? Why are they so Popular among Intelligent Well-Educated People? Why is our Elected King the Premier Author in the Whole World? Why do you Contradict yourself with your Ridiculous Arguments, which would never Hold Up in a Courtroom with a Righteous Judge in Charge of it? Why do you not Agree with me — that no such Capitalist JUNK is Needed for True Prosperity? But, if it is Needed, we can Produce it after everyone in the World is Living within **"Beautiful Swanky PALACES!" (A New Concept in Living Habits — Swanky Palaces for Poor People!) By The Worldwide People's Revolution!®** Book 066. Therefore, YOU are the "NUT," or Crazy Person, who needs to Learn HOW to Capitalize all such Important Words within your own Mind, whereby they have Double and even Triple Meanings. For Example, a Poor Person is not just Financially Poor; but, he or she is also Mentally, Spiritually, Physically, and Materially Poor with a Capital P, as in Extremely POOR! Therefore, it is now Time to Capitalize *"The Love of All that is GOOD,"* above the Love of Money, which is **"The Root Cause for almost all Evils"** (Book 078) in this World of Woes.

15-10 [_] O Adolf, I must Confess that all of the Best Arguments are in your Favor, which is also the Reason that many People do not Like you: beCause they cannot Rationally Justify their False Beliefs, which makes them Angry with you, if not Envious of you. After all, the Vast Majority of the People in this World of Wonders just Happen to AGREE with you and your Selected King, who is in Deed the Premier Author in the World, even if his Inspired Books are not Found in every House in the World, in all Major Languages in each House, as they could be: beCause each House could have a Special Spacious Stone Dome called, "The Swanky Truth-brary," as Opposed to the Public LIE-brary. Yes, it would become the most Used Room in the entire Stone Dome Home Complex, having no less than 60 Complete Editions of each Book in 60 Languages: because each Book will have to be Updated no less than 60 Times — after your Selected King Writes 300 more of them — just to get the Proper References to all of them within each Book. For Example, how many People have Heard of: **"HOW to Get our PRIORITIES in ORDER!" (The Glories of Democracy; and, Does Demon-ocracy have its Priorities in Order?) By The Reverend Doctor Billy Graham, Junior!**, Book 060? Indeed, if it were not Listed here, WHO would Discover it? †§‡

(HOW to be Liberated from all Slavery, Worldwide!)

— Chapter 16 —

Countless Books for Sale!

16-01 [_] Well, beCause of **"The Nature of CAPITALISM,"** (Book 038), most People have been "Programed" to Reject all such "References" to any such Books, as if they were nothing more than Advertisements for more Books for Sale, which is often the Case, and Certainly the Case in all of my Literature: beCause my Main Objective is to SELL more and more Books: beCause it is Necessary that I should have no less than 20 Trillion Dollars, just to Pay Off the National Debt of **"The Divided States of United Lies,"** which I will be Happy to do, if I can Sell that many Books! However, knowing the Nature of most People, and how they would Prefer to Eat a single Meal of Dog Food and/or Hog Slop, rather than Buy a Book to Read, the Chances of me Selling even a Million Copies of any given Book is very Slender — that is, UNLESS the Minds of the Masses of People are Suddenly Enlightened by the Bright Shining Light of Provable Truths within the Inspired Books of our Selected King. Yes, just ONE of his Enlightening Books could Spark a Forest Fire of Burning Truths, which would Consume all other Books, even as a Forest Fire Consumes all Trash and Firetrap Wooden / Plastic Houses that might get in the Way of it! Yes, once the Fire of Provable Truths is Burning in this very "Dry Forest," there will be no Stopping it: beCause of the Intense HEAT that is Generated by the Great ANGER of the Masses of People, who will be Ready and Willing to BURN DOWN all of those Cities of Confusion, which are Designed just for that Purpose — to go Up in Great Billowing Black Clouds of Toxic SMOKE — that is, UNLESS those Edomite Bankers Decide to COOPERATE with us Education Slaves, Work Slaves, Tax Slaves, Interest Slaves, Insurance Slaves, Drug Slaves, Rent Slaves, and Endless Bills Slaves, who are SICK of their Legal Robberies, who are Ready to REBEL, and Establish a NEW RIGHTEOUS One-World GovernMINT, which simply Mints and Prints the Necessary Brand New Money with Brand New Faces and Numbers, for the Purpose of HIRING whomever is Willing and Able to Learn and Work, for the Purpose of Building BEAUTIFUL Planned City States, which are Designed for TRUE Peace and TRUE Prosperity with Eternal Employment! Yes, just Think, O Tax Slaves, HOW could anyone be Poor, Hungry, Destitute, Homeless, or Miserable, if all People had Beautiful Stone Dome Home Complexes with Home-craft Workshops, Well-made Tools, Sales Shops, Luscious All-Mineral Organic Gardens, Vineyards, Orchards, Walk-in Coolers, Freezers, Ice Houses, Bat House Domes, Honeybee Domes, Churches, Mosques, Synagogues, Temples, Cathedrals, Concert Halls, Theaters, Gymnasiums, Auditoriums, Tennis Courts, Bowling Alleys, Indoor Swimming Pools, Game Rooms, and whatever they are Willing to WORK for? Yes, they could be Contented with nothing more than their Beautiful Stone Dome Home Complexes with their Gardens and Workshops, and never be Unemployed again, and never be anyone's Slave again: beCause of being FREE to Manage their own Lives as Independent Jackasses. However, People are Communal Creatures, who Require more than just Foods and Drinks, even though the Apostle Paul Commanded the Ministers to be Contented with Foods and Clothing, alone. {See *First Timothy 6* in: **"For the Love of Money!" (The Strange Things that People Say and Do to Get more Money!) By The Worldwide People's Revolution!®** Book 003.}

16-02 [_] O Adolf, there you go again, Advertising another Book for Sale! WHERE will it End?

16-03 [_] Well, why would you Want it to End? Indeed, I have Heard that you have a Million or more Unanswered Questions, which Answers can only be Found in a Swanky TRUTH-brary! Therefore, do not Allow yourself to Think of that Truth-brary as another EVIL Capitalist RIP-OFF: beCause nothing in this World is more Precious than the Inspired Words of Provable Truths! Therefore, Teach yourself to LOVE all such Good Books, just by READING them, which will Inspire you to get your Priorities in ORDER. After all, who is it that does not have Space in their House of Love for 300 Inspired Books, which can be Obtained for FREE! Yes, if you People Act Wisely, and Elect our Selected King to be your Righteous KING, he will Provide all of those Inspired Books in the Swanky Truth-brary for FREE to everyone who Qualifies, and Wants a Leather-bound Copy of them. Indeed, they will come in Beautiful Hand-carved Leather-bound Volumes of 10 or so Books under one Cover! Yes, they will be LARGE Books with Heavy-duty Leather Covers, which are Designed to Endure the Test of Time, which you can spread out on a Special Hand-crafted Movable Wooden Table, which is Designed to Accommodate your Swanky Easy Chair, which is Designed to be Extremely Comfortable, which you will also be able to Sleep in when it is laid back: beCause, in Order to get the Most Enlightenment from any Book, your Body and Mind needs lots of REST and Sufficient SLEEP, which you can Obtain while your Garden Plants are Growing. Therefore, just RELAX, and take your Sweet Time to Study those Good Books: beCause they make Good Entertainment, while they are Enlightening your Mind, which will Inspire you to make your own Carved, Leather-bound Books for Sale, and for a Good Profit, which you can do while Sitting in a Swanky Easy Chair, using another Special Movable Table with Carving Tools, whereby you will be Able to Earn no less than 40$ per Hour, once you get the "Hang" of it, whereby you will easily be Able to Afford to Buy whatever Musical Instruments that you might Want to Play, as well as go on Swanky Vacations to other **"GLORIOUS Swanky Hotels Castles and Fortresses!"** †§‡

16-04 [_] O Adolf, you "Paint" an almost Unbelievable "Picture" for us to Believe in, which is a bit Confusing to me. For Example, HOW will I be Able to Afford to Buy that First Swanky Easy Chair, which would Cost no less than five thousand Dollars — that is, IF the Heavy-duty Leather is CARVED with Pretty Flowers, Animals, Leaves, and whatever, on the Sides and Back of the Chair; but, not on the Seat, nor on the Arms of the Chair: beCause that would be too Rough for Delicate Spoiled Children, who would have to have Custom-made Easy Chairs with at least 6 inches of Padding, or Foam Rubber? †§‡

16-05 [_] Well, it only Sounds Confusing to you: beCAUSE you have not Studied all of the Inspired Books in the Swanky TRUTH-brary. Yes, I would also be Confused, if I did not already Know the Answers for all such Important Questions, which I have Discovered by Reading those Exceptionally Good Books, which should be Mandatory Reading in all Public Schools, Worldwide. Yes, they should be Translated into all Major Languages: so that everyone can Study them: beCause they have nothing Better to Do, now that most of them are Unemployed, Broke, and near unto Homelessness. Indeed, they have been Hoping to Discover GOOD Jobs with HIGH Wages; but, for every such Job Opening, there are a thousand or more People Lined Up to get it. Indeed, that will not be the Case when we begin to Build those **"GLORIOUS Swanky Hotels Castles and Fortresses"**: because there will Suddenly be an Abundance of Jobs with Good Swanky Wages, which will be Begging for Working Soldiers to Collect all such Wages. Therefore, the entire False Economy will be Transformed into a very Prosperous Crime-free Economy: beCause everyone will have LOTS of Money, if they are Willing to Work for it; and,

(HOW to be Liberated from all Slavery, Worldwide!)

they will be more than Willing: beCause they will be INSPIRED with Great Enthusiasm; but, only AFTER they have Learned HOW to Fast and Pray, whereby the Poisons and Filth and Drugs within their Bodies will be Eliminated, whereby their Natural JOY and Happiness will Fill their Souls with Enthusiasm for Constructing those Beautiful Planned City States. ‡ (See Verse 09-03.)

16-06 [_] O Adolf, it all Sounds very Good; but, in Reality, those Lying Edomite Bankers Control the Money Supply and the entire Great False Economy. Therefore, we will need someone like you to Arrest them, bring them to Court, and Prove them to be Guilty of High Crimes in Low Places, whereby they will either REPENT and Change their Ways, or else be put OUT of Business! Yes, they should all be Baked in NAZI Ovens, as you Suggested 11-03, if they do not Confess all of their Monetary Sins, and come Clean with us Usury Slaves. †§‡

16-07 [_] Well, if enough of our Selected King's Inspired Books get Sold and "Red" by the Masses of People, we will not have to Boil anyone in Used Motor Oil, nor Bake them in any Nazi Crematory Ovens: beCause we Education Slaves, Work Slaves, Tax Slaves, Usury Slaves, Interest Slaves, Drug Slaves, Insurance Slaves, Debt Slaves, Rent Slaves, Gas Slaves, Water Bills Slaves, Sex Slaves, and Childcare Slaves will simply go to Bed, come next April 21st, and SLEEP! Yes, we will Patiently Wait on the Democratic Governments of all Wise Nations to DEMAND: **"The Great Worldwide TELEVISED Court HEARING,"** whereby we might Learn the Whole Truth about all Kinds of Important Subjects, including that of a GOOD Economy, which is Based on the Principle that everyone on this Earth Needs to EAT and DRINK, while Living in SECURE Stone Dome Home Complexes, which are Designed for LIVING, which are Connected with Luscious All-Mineral Organic Gardens, Vineyards, Orchards, Elevators, Electric Subway Trains, HUGE half-million-gallon Cisterns for Water Storage, Home-craft Workshops, Sales Shops, Cathedrals, Temples, Mosques, Synagogues, Churches, Basilicas, Theaters, Gymnasiums, Swimming Pools, Tennis Courts, Bowling Alleys, Ice-skating Rinks, Roller Skating Rinks, and whatever the People are Willing and Able to WORK for, by Means of: **"Seven Great Armies of Working Soldiers,"** who may be Drafted into such Armies, if they do not Willingly Volunteer, after Learning about those GOOD Swanky Wages — such as 60$ per Hour for Setting a certain Amount of Ceramic Tiles on Concrete Cistern Walls. Yes, just after Fresh Clean AIR to Breathe, People Need to have Good Reliable Water Supplies of LIVING Water to Drink and Water their Gardens, plus Wholesome Natural Foods to Eat, Proper Natural Clothing to Wear, and SECURE Terrorist-proof Houses to Live in! ‡ {See www.Amazon.com for: **"A List of FAIR Swanky Wages!" (The Equitable Wage System!) By The Worldwide People's Revolution!® Book 065.**}

16-08 [_] O Adolf, if it is just a Matter of Selling Books, in Order to bring all of that about, I would like to Volunteer, right now. However, being a Church Mouse, I am too Poor to Afford to Buy even 10 Copies of this Inspired Book to Sell to anyone, even if I can Keep 90% of the Net Profits!

16-09 [_] Well, in your Case, as a very Poor Church Mouse, you must Act Wisely, and set a Trap for the Pastor of your Church, who might be Baited and Enticed to Read this Book, or some other Inspired Book by our Selected King, and thus be "Tempted" to Read more of his Inspired Books, until at last, with your Urging him on, he Decides to Read Aloud all such Books to his entire Congregation, who must be Encouraged to Invite non-members to Attend all such

Meetings of the Minds, whereby a Great Controversy can get going, and Spread itself like a Great Forest Fire throughout all American Cities, which will be Heated Up by News Reports about it, which will Draw more People into the "Trap," from which they will not be Able to Escape: beCause that is the Nature of Provable Truths; but, ONLY when those Truths are Shared with a certain Number of Intelligent People, who can COUNT THE COST of the Rejection of all such Provable Truths, which is UTTER DESTRUCTION! Yes, it will be the END of Babylon — the END of Confusion: beCause the Light of Truths will be Shining Brightly into all Corners of the House of Hate, where not even a single Church Mouse can Hide!

16-10 [_] O Adolf, I must Confess that your Head is Filled with Visions of Sugar Plums and Wishful Dancing Dreams: beCause there is no Way on this Earth that any Preacher is going to be Interested in putting himself OUT of Business! Indeed, he, like all other Professional Capitalists, are Greatly THREATENED by any Provable Truths, which they might have to Confess: beCause no one can Rightly Argue Against any such Truths, which Causes Great Frustrations within their Minds: beCause they are Seeking to Justify the EVILS of Capitalism, including the EVILS of those Lying Edomites on Wall Street, in New Yuck City, which is one of the Major Edomite Hubs on the World Wheels of Capitalism, which is a Wagon Train that runs around the World, you might say, which Runs Rough-shod over whomever Resists it, and Tramples them Under: beCause we are of a Lower Order than Lying Edomites, who can get by with almost any Evil Action, even though I have a certain HOPE that it will not always be that Way.

— Chapter 17 —

Will the Lying Edomites Slip Through the Net that is Spread Out for them?

17-01 [_] Well, when one Considers the Fact that those Lying Edomites Control the News Media, the Major Book Publishing Companies in New York City, Hollywood Nonsense, Medical Scams, Major Drug Companies, Weapons Manufacturing, Chemical Corporations, and all Major Banks, Worldwide, it is not Difficult to Understand that our "Best Friend" is the INTERNET, which they would also like to Control; but, as of this Date, they have not yet Managed to take Away that Freedom, whereby we, the Masses of People, still have some Control over them: because of our Freedom of Speech, which is Limited by the Scope or Reach of it, which is normally Confined to our own little Worlds, you might say: beCause few of us have Sufficient Money for Advertising all such Books on TV and Radio Networks. In Fact, if we are to Overcome the BEAST, we must Unite our Efforts, Pool our Resources, and Work Together on it: because no Independent Jackass is going to Accomplish it. †§‡ {See www.Amazon.com for: **"The Loathsome Burdens of the Independent Jackasses!" (A New Approach for Solving our Massive Problems!) By The Dictator — Adolf Hitler, Junior!** Book 051.}

17-02 [_] O Adolf, your so-called "Net" has been Constructed; but, it appears that no one is Strong Enough to LIFT IT UP, seeing that such a Courageous Person would have to read no less

(HOW to be Liberated from all Slavery, Worldwide!)

than 50 Inspired Books, just to get a Good Hold on it. Therefore, what are the Chances of Spreading it out, all around the World? †‡

17-03 [_] Well, it would not be the First Time in World History that an Inspired Book got Published; but, it will be the First Time in World History that all such Inspired Books have Sold BILLIONS of Copies! Indeed, only the *Holy Bible* comes close to Competing with that, and only beCause of having a Multitude of Translations, including that of our Selected King, whose New MAGNIFIED Version (NMV) is by Far the Most Popular: beCause it is Understandable. †§‡ {See the above Link for: **"Thu Nq MAGNUFIID Verzhun uv Thu PROVERBZ uv KING SOLUMUN in Plaan Ingglish!"** (The Understandable Version of the Famous Proverbs of King Solomon in Plain English!), Book 028, plus: **"ECCLESIASTES UNCOVERED!"** (The New MAGNIFIED Version of Ecclesiastes and the Song of Solomon in Plain English!), Book 034, which will give to you Good Examples of what it Means to MAGNIFY all such Truths, whereby they become Understandable.}

17-04 [_] O Adolf, is your Selected King not ADDING a lot of LIES to the *Scriptures* by Magnifying the Truths within them? †§‡§§

17-05 [_] Well, do you Believe that a Gemstone is Defiled by Cutting and Polishing it, whereby a very Rough Rock can be made into a Beautiful Thing that is Admired by all Honest People? Please check out the Cover Photo for: **"Are you a Jobless Graduate of the SKQL uv FQLZ?"** (HOW to get a GOUD EJUKAASHUN without Robbing the Bank!), Book 020, which shows a Beautiful Onyx Vase with many Striations in Various Colors, which Rock would hardly Attract the Attention of anyone, if it were not Cut and Polished. Likewise, the *Scriptures* are like very Rough Gemstones, which have been "Cut and Polished" by Countless Preachers, Priests, Professors, Politicians, and Teachers, who have Produced Multitudes of Sermons and Speeches, which have Greatly Enriched the World. However, a Great King must be Crowned with the Gemstones of Provable Truths, which have been Highly Polished: so that they Sparkle in the Light of Good Understanding, which is WHY all such Great Kings must be Honored for it, who are Exceptional People — such as our Selected King, who is the King of the Birds, you might say, whose Tale of Truths Changes Colors, According to the Intensity of the Light that is Shined on it, which can be Shined on it by any Preacher, Priest, Professor, Politician, or Teacher who has been Enlightened by that Awesome Tale of Provable Truths. {See www.Amazon.com for: **"An Amazing Collection of Wit and Wisdom!"** (The Marvelous Tale of the Colorful Peacock from Angel Ridge, and the Strong Rope of Everlasting Hope!) By The Worldwide People's Revolution!®, Book 048, which contains a Famous Document called: **"The KO$T of a DIPSTIK!"**}

17-06 [_] O Adolf, I would Bet that those Lying Edomites did not Expect such a Unique Person as your Selected King to Arise among them, having a Good Command of the *Scriptures,* whereby they are not Able to "Pull the Wool over his Eyes," you might say. Indeed, those Lying Edomites likely Imagined that they got by, scot-free: because X-amount of Professing "Christians" Stand with them, and even Support the Israelis, as if they were the Chosen Seeds of Israel, when Father Jacob would Naturally Deny that they have any Spiritual Relationship at all: because they are Possessed by Evil Spirits, even as Esau was Possessed, whom God Hated, according to *Romans 9:13, KJV,* which is likely the Truth: beCause God Hates ALL that is Evil:

beCause he is All that is GOOD. Therefore, if those Israelis want to Prove that they are the Children of Israel, they will have REPENT with True Repentance. {See: **"HOW to Become a HOLY Man!" (40 Good Reasons WHY People Should FAST and PRAY!)**, Book 045, which is a Companion Book of: **"The Proper RULES for FASTING!" (The Complete Instruction Manual for True Repentance!) By The Worldwide People's Revolution!® Book 046.**}

17-07 [_] Well, many People would Argue with you about that, seeing that God Supposedly Created ALL Things, including those Hateful Mosquitoes, which Inflict Various Diseases in People, whereby Millions of them DIE from those Diseases, which does not seem to be GOOD to anyone, and especially to those People who must Suffer and Die from Malaria, for Example. However, the Confusion arises from a Missing WORD in the *Bible*. *"In the Beginning were the Words of Truths, and the Words of Truths were with God, and the Words of Truths are Gods. Indeed, these same Words were in the Beginning with God, who is All that is Good. All Good Things were Created by the Gods, and without them was not any Good Thing made that was made: because, in them is Life, Power, and Great Glory, which is also the Life and Enlightenment of Mankind; and thus the Light Shines in the Darkness of Ignorance; but, the Darkness of Ignorance cannot Comprehend it: beCause the Spiritual Eyes are Blinded by such Bright Light, being Accustomed to the Darkness of Ignorance. Nevertheless, it shall come to pass during the Last Days, when the Darkness of Ignorance will be Extremely Intense, that the Master Farmer will Raise Up a Special Servant, whom many Deceived People will Imagine is just another Ignorant Fool, like themselves, who will be put to Open Shame by his Sharp Sword of Divine Truths, which will Separate the Truths from the Lies, and make all Spiritual Things easy for Wise Obedient People to Understand, who will Demand* **'The Great Worldwide TELEVISED Court HEARING,'** *whereby those Lying Edomites will be Summoned to Court, and Proven to be Guilty of Various Kinds of Lies, Deceptions, and Frauds. Yes, you shall Live to See it for yourself, O Righteous Man, if you just Cling to the Rope of Hope with both Hands, and Wrap yourself up in it, and put your Confidence in it: because only the Sword of Truths can Liberate you from the Prison of Lies. Therefore, do not put your Trust in any Ignorant Fool; but, put your Trust in Provable Truths, which will Liberate you from Education Slavery, Work Slavery, Tax Slavery, Usury Slavery, Insurance Slavery, Drug Slavery, Sex Slavery, Childcare Slavery, Endless Bills Slavery, and all other Kinds of Slavery; but, only IF — only on the CONDITION, that you Elect a Righteous KING to Manage that Court Hearing, who has Authority over ALL of the People: so that he can Order those Wicked Edomites to Answer his Important Questions, or else be Boiled in HOT Oil, Feet First, until they Learn to SPEAK when Asked such Important Questions, whereby Peace can be Established among all Nations, who must Learn the WHOLE Truth about those White Jews and Edomites, who have always been Chief Enemies: beCause they were Born that Way from the Womb of Rebekah, who Married Isaac for his Wealth, and not for his Good Health, even though he was the Healthiest Person that she ever Met, whom she Learned to Love for his Goodness, whose Goodness was Inherited by Jacob, while the Evilness of Rebekah was Inherited by Esau, who had the Great Disadvantage of being an Ugly Baby, who was not Favored by Rebekah, as was Jacob, whom she also Learned to Love more and more: because he Inherited the Goodness of Isaac and Abraham, who never had a Selfish Greedy Bone in his entire Body, you might say. Yes, there were Major Differences between those Twin Brothers: beCause they were Born for Different Purposes; and thus Esau became the Father of the Edomites, whose Descendants became the Chief Scribes and Pharisees during the Time of Jesus Christ, who also Hated him without any Justifiable Causes, who*

Orchestrated his Arrest, False Trial, and Crucifixion: beCause they Envied him for his Goodness, and for his Popularity among the Masses of People, who Loved him for his Miracles and Generosities; but, behold, they will Live again, during the Last Days, whereby they will be brought to Perfection in their Wickedness, being Chief Bankers, Lawyers, Politicians, Doctors, Professors, Chemists, and Inventors of Abominations: beCause they Inherited all such Evil Spirits, which will be Passed Down from Generation to Generation, until at Last they will be brought to Trials for their Evils: because it will be Demanded of them by the Masses of People, who will Learn all about their Wickedness by Means of the Internet, whereby Freedom of Speech will still be Permissible, whereby the Light of Truths can Disperse the Darkness of Ignorance. And thus it shall be: beCause the Master Farmer and Chief Architect has Spoken it. Amen." †§‡

17-08 [_] O Adolf, have you gone MAD? Are you a Distant Relative of MuhamMAD, himself? Are you not Aware that those Lying Edomites will have you Crucified for telling all such Truths? †§‡

17-09 [_] Well, I am quite Aware of their Powers. However, you must Remember that I have Woven a Net to Trap them, like X-amount of Fishes in the Sea, whereby none of them will Escape, even if they Die before that Great Meeting of the Most Intelligent Minds: beCause, from that Time Forward, whenever any Lying Edomite Arises with his or her False Accusation, such a Person will be taken to COURT, and made to Prove it. In other Words, they will not be Allowed to get by with Telling such Lies, even in Printed Books. After all, Books are Sacred Things, which should be Respected for their Provable Truths, whereby Children and Adults can have Confidence in them, which would especially be True of the *Holy Bible*, which is a Mutilated book of books, which I just Proved in the Quotation from *the New MAGNIFIED Version of John 1*, which left OUT the Word, GOOD, as in *"All Good Things."* †§‡

17-10 [_] O Adolf, Verse 17-07 did not Contain any Quotation from any Bible; but, it did seem to be much more Accurate, according to the Realities of Life, than anything in *the Book of Saint John*, which can be Proven in a Courtroom. *"And the Gods said, 'Let us make Mankind in OUR Images.' And thus the Gods Created Mankind in their own Images, being Males and Freemales, who are Free from all Judgments so long as they Love and Obey their Husbands."* — *The NMV of Genesis 1:26*. Selah. †§‡

— Chapter 18 —

ORDER in the COURT!

18-01 [_] Are you Lying Edomites Prepared to Answer the Important Questions that shall be Asked by our Selected King at: **"The Great Worldwide TELEVISED Court HEARING!" (That Great Meeting of the Most Intelligent and Well-Educated Minds)**? If not, speak up!

A-[_] I Agree, they should Answer those Important Questions.

B-[_] I Disagree, they should not have to Answer any Important Questions: beCause this is a Kangaroo Court for Believers, only; and not a Real Trial of any Kind.

C-[_] I Confess that all such Liars should be brought to Court, and made to Prove that they are Worthy to Control the News Media, the Major Banks, the Federal Government, the Medical Establishment, the Drug Industries, the Insurance Corporations, and the entire Military Industrial Congressional Bankers' Drug Cartel Complex.

D-[_] Damned if I will ever Check the C Box with an X: beCause I am another Lying Edomite, who does not have the Faith of a Dimwitcrat.

E-[_] Educated People Know for a Fact that there are many "Breeds" of Edomites, including those who Call themselves Jews, who are NOT True Jews, neither in their Hearts, nor in their Attitudes. Otherwise, they would be Happy to Check the Appropriate Boxes with Statements that they Agree with. (See *Revelation 2:9 and 3:9, KJV.*)

F-[_] I Fail to Understand what this Trial is all about. However, I will still be Bold enough to Check the Boxes with Statements that I Agree with, and with a Lead Pencil: so that just in case I Change my Mind, I can Erase the Check Mark, or X, and thus Correct it without making a Fool of myself at some Future Trial for Chief Fools.

G-[_] God Knows that you are an Innocent Ignorant Soul, while a Lying Edomite is a Wicked Person, who Knows for a Fact that he or she is on the WRong Side, if he or she Opposes **"The Swanky Sword of Divine Truths!" (The Most Powerful Weapon in the Whole Universe!)**, which is otherwise known as: **"The Sharp Sword of Provable Truths!" By The Worldwide People's Revolution!® Book 067.**

H-[_] Honest People will not be Afraid to Check any Appropriate Boxes with an X: because they have not Committed any Crimes, whereby they might be Convicted and Sentenced to spend Time in a Prison for it, or otherwise be Punished by some other Means, by the Vote of the Jury, who can be the Masses of People, Worldwide, in this Case: beCause of the Convenience of Computers and the Internet, which can have all of our Selected King's Inspired Books Posted on the Internet with Boxes to be Checked by all Wise Readers, whose Check Marks will be used to Liberate them during the Judgment

(HOW to be Liberated from all Slavery, Worldwide!)

Day, when God Opens up all of the Inspired Books for Judging us, even as it is Written in the *Holy Bible*, in *the Book of Revelation.* †‡

I-[_] Innocent People will not Participate in any such Surveys of our Values: because they have too much to Hide from the Federal Government, which would be Revealed if they should Expose themselves by Checking the Boxes with Statements that they Agree with, in: **"The Complete SURVEYS of our VALUES!" (SURVEYS of Religious Spiritual Political Governmental Sexual Social Moral Economic Business Labor Habitual and Miscellaneous VALUES!) By The Worldwide People's Revolution!®** Book 059. †§§

J-[_] Justice Demands that those Lying Edomites should be Summoned to Court, and made to Answer the Important Questions.

K-[_] King Jesus will Summon them to Court during his Great Day of Judgment.

L-[_] Lots of Laughs! King Jesus is a Jewish MYTH, and not a Real Person, much less the Son of God: beCause God does not have a Son, much less a Chosen Son. Indeed, if you Doubt it, just Ask any Honest Muslim. †§‡

M-[_] Muslims are Insane: beCause they Believe in MuhamMAD, who was a Murderous Adulterous Lying Son of SATAN, himself, who said that all of the Infidels should be KILLED by Muslims, which is what ISIS Believes, who Chop Off Christians' Heads, and do other very Mean Things to them. †‡

N-[_] Not everyone Swallows all such Propaganda: because it is Pure Nonsense! Indeed, ISIS is the Israeli Secret Instigation Service, which was Established to Inspire more Wars: because it is Extremely Profitable for Israeli and American Weapons Manufacturers, whose Chief Executive Officers are mostly Lying Edomites from Niggerville, N.Y.! †§‡

O-[_] Are there no OPTIONS? Can we Tax Slaves and Potential War Victims not DEMAND **"The Great Worldwide TELEVISED Court HEARING,"** whereby we might Learn the Whole Truth about them, and thus bring this Madness to an END!?

P-[_] Most People will Agree with you: because it is now Possible to Hold such a Great Meeting of the Most Intelligent Minds, which can especially use the YouTube Videos, which Expose those Lying Edomites. (Search for *Benjamin Freedman,* for Example.)

Q-[_] The Great Question is this: **"Will we Education Slaves, Work Slaves, Tax Slaves, Interest Slaves, Insurance Slaves, Drug Slaves, and Endless Bills Slaves DEMAND that Great Meeting of the Most Intelligent Minds; or, will we sit around and do nothing, until Atomic and Hydrogen Bombs Fall on us??"**

R-[_] It is REVIVAL Time, when all Wise Preachers, Priests, Professors, Politicians, Teachers, Authors, News Reporters, and Educated People should take up Reading ALOUD in Public Places all of our Selected King's Inspired Books to as many People as Possible for Stirring Up a Great REVOLUTION — such as the World has never Seen before, whereby all Evil People can be put OUT of Business, whereby Goodness can Overcome Evilness, and thus we can Establish a New Renaissance, and thus take up our Hammers and Chisels for Carving out New and Beautiful Artistic Swanky Fortresses, whereby the Saints would Arise with Great Rejoicing! †

S-[_] Senator Slimeball Slippery Slopinheimer will never allow it: because he Works for the Lying Edomite Bankers, who Control the Money Supply, who Control the Great False Economy, who can Make or Break us: because that is HOW they have Set it Up for themselves, whereby the Rich People get Richer, and the Poor People get Poorer. ‡

T-[_] Tally Ho, Mates, it is now Time for a First Class REVOLUTION, which can Begin by going to Bed, come next April 21st, whereby we Consumers STOP Buying their TRASH and Drugs, which will Cause them to Yield to **"The Swanky Sword of Divine Truths!"** Book 067.

U-[_] I Understand what you are saying. However, if we do not Persuade the Vast Majority of the People to Cooperate with us, such an Act will have very little if any Effect. Therefore, it is very Important that almost everyone, Worldwide, should Learn about **"The Great Worldwide TELEVISED Court HEARING,"** whereby they might ALL go to Bed, and STAY in Bed, until all Governments YIELD to the Sword of Truths! Yes, it will Require FAITH in the Inspired Words of our Selected King, even if he Dies from a Broken Heart! After all, he has been Patiently Waiting for our Cooperation for more than 40 Years!

V-[_] The Victory will be to those Wise People, who not only Learn about that Great Meeting of the Most Intelligent and Well-Educated Minds; but, who also Promote it into Reality: beCause it is the One and ONLY Bloodless Revolutionary Plan, which no Leaders of any Nations will be Able to Resist: beCause they all Want TRUE JUSTICE, which Begins with Learning the WHOLE Truth, whatever it might be, which is all that we Tax Slaves are Interested in: beCause we are SICK of all of those Edomite LIES. Therefore, come next April 21st, we must all become Extremely SICK of them. †§‡

W-[_] Why Wait until next April 21st to have a Revolution? Why not get on with it right away, without Reading ANY of your Selected King's Inspired Books: so that our Swords of Truths are very DULL and Ineffective? †§‡§§

X-[_] X-amount of People would say that you are CRAZY! However, we all Desperately Need to Sharpen up our Swords of Truths by Studying your Selected King's Good Books, whereby we can Answer all of the Important Questions that People might Ask, whereby we can put their Minds at Ease!

Y-[_] I Refuse to Yield to any such Temptations to Read any of your Selected King's Uninspired Books: beCause I might have to Change my Ways of Living, which would Prove to be too Humiliating for me: beCause I am another Lying Edomite! †§‡§§

Z-[_] Even a Stubborn Zebra can Change his Ways of Living, if he Moves into a Swanky Fortress with other Zebras: because there will be no more Lions nor Laughing Hyenas

(HOW to be Liberated from all Slavery, Worldwide!)

among them. Indeed, they can Stop Fighting each other, and Rest in Peace under the Shade of Mango Trees, Date Palms, Grape Vines and Fig Trees, along with those Wildebeests and Water Buffaloes, who are likely Tired of Running Away from their Enemies with the Deers and Antelopes. Yes, it is now Time for all of them to Rest in Peace, and get some Zzz!

18-02 [_] I Object, your Honor: beCause I am NOT a Lying Edomite. Therefore, I do not have to Answer any of your Questions, nor anyone else's Questions.

18-03 [_] And WHY do you Object to Answering any Important Questions, if you are not a Lying Edomite?

> A-[_] I Agree, if he or she is NOT a Lying Edomite, he or she should be Willing and Ready to Answer any Important Questions, even if only to say: "I Honestly do not Know the Answer to that Question, your Honor."

> B-[_] I Believe that everyone should Answer the Questions that are Asked of them, even if they Incriminate themselves: beCause they can be and should be Forgiven, if they Repent.

> C-[_] I Confess that it is Possible for a Person to be Incriminated by a Wily Lawyer, even if he or she is Innocent. For Example, a Foxy Porcupine Lawyer might ask a Horny Young Man, "At what Time of the Night did you begin to Masturbate yourself?" Yes, that Lawyer would Know for a Fact that Horny Hairy was Masturbating himself, almost every Night: because his Bedroom Smelled like Sperm; and therefore, Horny Hairy would Appear to be Guilty, in spite of the Fact that it is no Sin to Masturbate yourself. Indeed, there is no Commandment against it in the entire Bible, nor even any Suggestion that a Person might go to Hell for doing it; but, Thanks to False Religions, many Young Men are Guilt-Ridden for doing it, which has Driven some of them Crazy, who have even Castrated themselves! Yes, Guilt can Drive anyone Crazy. ‡

> D-[_] Dumbmocracy never Mentions Masturbation: beCause almost everyone does it in Secret, which makes it Shameful. However, that is not to say that everyone should be doing it in Public Places, nor even behind Dumpsters: because it is Disgraceful.

> E-[_] Educated People know that it is Possible for a Wicked Lawyer to Arrange his Questions in such a Way as to make People Feel Guilty, and also Look Guilty; but, in the Case of those Lying Edomites, they will be Asked Simple Questions that anyone could Answer without any Shame. For Example, "Do you Sincerely Believe that 4 or 5 Adult Bodies could be Stuffed into just one Nazi Crematory Oven at one Time, seeing that the Doorway is only 18 inches Wide and 20 inches High, which has to also Accommodate the Steel Gurney, which is 4 inches High?" [_] Yes; or, [_] No.

> F-[_] I Failed to Check either Box above in Verse E: because I am Afraid that I might Incriminate myself in your Selected King's Courtroom.

G-[_] God knows that you have already Incriminated yourself by NOT Checking the Yes or No Boxes: beCause even a Child could use a Measuring Stick to Discover whether or not 4 or 5 Adult Bodies could be put through such a Small Hole at one Time, being Stacked Up on a Steel Gurney that is only 18 inches Wide. Therefore, you are Guilty by Reason of your Unwarranted Fears: beCause there is nothing to Fear by Telling the Truth about whatever you Sincerely Believe.

H-[_] I am Honest enough to Answer that Question in Verse E: because I do not Fear that I will be Proven to be WRong in any Courtroom. Moreover, I also Checked the G and H Boxes with an X.

I-[_] I am Ignorant, and therefore Innocent by Reason of my Ignorance. Therefore, I have no Idea whether or not 4 or 5 Adult Bodies could be Stuffed through a Doorway that is only 18 inches Wide and 20 inches High: beCause it could be that the Gurneys for Carrying the Bodies into the Retorts were each 30 feet Long. Therefore, that is what I Believe: because that Edomite Lie seems to Answer the Question. †§‡§§

J-[_] Justice Demands that your Lying Tongue should be Cut Out: beCause no one has ever Testified that those Nazi Metal Gurneys at the Crematoriums were more than 7 feet Long, much less Retorts that were 30+ feet Long. Therefore, you should Study those Photos of the Nazi Crematoriums on the Internet, which Clearly Reveal that they were Normal Traditional German Crematoriums, which had ONE Chimney for 3 Retorts, and no more. Indeed, each of the 2 Crematoriums in Auschwitz contained only 3 Ovens, where 1 to 3 Bodies were Cremated at one Time, which took from 4 to 12 Hours: beCause it Required no less than 1 Hour just to Heat Up the Ovens, and 2 to 10 Hours to Cremate the Bodies, depending on their Sizes, Ages, Weather Conditions, etc., and one more Hour to Cool Off the Ovens before the Doors could Safely be Opened, which can be and must be and will be Proven in a Courtroom for all People to Witness, whereby Dead Hogs can take the Place of People, which will Simulate the Nazi Concentration Camp Crematories in Auschwitz, Poland, in 1944—1945. †§‡

K-[_] King Jesus would never Permit such a Demonstration in a Courtroom: beCause he would simply Forgive those Lying Edomites, who have Collected Billions of Dollars from the Germans for the Horrors of the Jewish Holocaust. †§‡

L-[_] Lots of Laughs! King Jesus would have those Lying Edomites Demonstrate just Exactly HOW 4 or 5 Bodies could have been Cremated in one Oven every 10 Minutes, as it states in no Uncertain Terms in the Holocaust Museum in Washington, or else he would have those Lying Edomites Stuffed into Nazi Ovens, until they Confessed the Truth of it, even if it Required a hundred Years to get such a Confession! †§‡§§

M-[_] If those Lying Edomites had enough MONEY, they could likely Bribe the Judge, and thus Skip Out of any Court Hearings. †§‡

N-[_] Nonsense! We would Elect a RIGHTEOUS Judge, who would be our Selected King, whom we Know we can Trust: beCause he is the Most Honest Person among us, who has Filled Out and Filed **"The Complete SURVEYS of our VALUES!"** Book 059.

(HOW to be Liberated from all Slavery, Worldwide!)

{See www.Amazon.com for: **"Mark Twain Races for the PRESIDENCY!"** (The 2020 Presidential Candidates Desperately Need Some STRONG Undefeatable COMPETITION!) By The Worldwide People's Revolution!® Book 033.}

O-[_] That is just your Honest OPINION, and not a Proven FACT. After all, I have never "red" so many LIES in my entire Life, as I have Found in his Uninspired Books! †§‡§§

P-[_] People the World over Know for a Fact that our Selected King is an Honest Person: beCause there is no Way on this Earth that anyone could Write 200 Inspired Books in less than 3 Years, unless he was and still is an Honest Person. †§‡

Q-[_] The Great Question is this: **"Will those Lying Edomites Appear in our Selected King's Courtroom, Willingly; or, will they have to be Arrested and Dragged into Court with Shackles and Chains on them??"**

R-[_] Righteous White Israelites will not Object to Appearing in any such Courtrooms: beCause they have nothing to HIDE. †‡

S-[_] I Know HOW to Solve this whole Thing without anyone going to Court! Indeed, all of those Lying Edomites can now begin to Write their Confessions in Books, which they can Publish for FREE on the Internet for everyone to Study, whereby they can be Forgiven for their many SINS; and then no one will be Wasting any Precious Time with all such Sarcastic Nonsense. †§‡

T-[_] No Time will be Wasted by Conducting that Great Meeting of the Most Intelligent Minds: beCause we will Discover many Truths that we never Heard before. Therefore, it is now Time to SHUT OFF all Television Channels, except for that one of **"The New RIGHTEOUS One-World Government,"** which will Televise the entire Meeting in all Major Languages, Worldwide. Yes, we will Discover whether or not Men Landed on the Moon, who Murdered President John Kennedy, who Bombed the Alfred P. Murrah Federal Building in Oklahoma City, and WHO Conspired to make Attacks on Iraq, and WHY they Conspired it, as well as WHO Conspired to Destroy so many Lives in New York City during September 11th, 2001, which still Remains a MYSTERY with 10,000 or more Unanswered Questions! For Example, "HOW could 283 Hardened Steel Columns COLLAPSE in Unison in World Trade Center 7 within less than 7 Seconds without the Assistance of TONS of EXPLOSIVES, which would have Required much Time to Set Up those Explosives in Advance?" †§‡ {See www.AE911TRUTH.org for: *Experts Speak Out*. Otherwise, Search for it on YouTube Videos, which presents several Versions to Choose from — from Minutes to Hours. Be Wise, and Chose the Longest one with the most Information, and be Alert, Attentive, Patient, and Persistent, whereby you will Finally Agree with the 3,000+ Architects and Engineers, who Agree with our Selected King, who Sensed the Truth of it in September of 2001, when the Media Networks only Presented Sensational Stories, and not Facts, nor Answers to Important Questions: because that is HOW all Criminals Attempt to Cover Up the Evidences by DIVERSIONS and DISTRACTIONS from the Evidences and Realities — such as nothing but a little Hole about 6 feet Deep, 20 feet Long and 10 feet Wide in the Ground near Shanksville,

Pennsylvania, when there should have been at least 2 Six-ton Titanium Jet Engines, Airplane Wings, Tail, Fuselage, Cockpit and other Airplane Parts lying all around, along with Dead Bodies, Luggage, Suitcases, Clothing, Seats, Telephones, and whatever those Passengers had brought with them, even as it was for all other similar Airplane Crashes in World History. But, behold, there was ZERO EVIDENCES of an Airplane Crash at that Site, except for those Airplane Parts that were Planted there in the Woods by the Conspirators. However, it did Appear that a Guided Missile had Struck in that Hole. ‡}

U-[_] I Understand that we must get down to the Roots of our Massive Problems, and Discover WHO is in Charge of this World of Woes, and get RID of them, which can Best be Done by Demanding: **"The Great Worldwide TELEVISED Court HEARING!"** ‡

V-[_] Vice President Blabbermouth probably knows who is in Charge: because he is Good Friends with those Lying Edomites. Therefore, he should be Asked some Important Questions at that Great Meeting of the Most Intelligent Minds. †§‡

W-[_] You People are Calling for World War 3! Indeed, it is the POPE of ROME who Controls this World of Woes, which is WHY he is not Afraid to Host **"The Great Worldwide TELEVISED Court HEARING"** in Saint Peter's Basilica: because he Controls all of the Puppet Strings! †§‡§§

X-[_] X-amount of Ignorant People Believe all such Edomite Lies; but, the Truth is that the Pope of Rome has very Limited Powers, or else he would Order that Great Meeting of the Most Intelligent Minds, himself, just to Discover the WHOLE Truth, whatever it might be. Moreover, if he does not Check the above Box with a Red X, he is Suspect of being another Lying Edomite, himself. Chances are that the Queen of England could tell us who the Real Criminals are, seeing that she is the Richest Person on the Earth. However, it is Illegal for her to Publically Express any of her Personal Political Beliefs about any Subject: beCause all Monarchs are supposed to be NEUTRAL, without any Political nor Religious Opinions about anything. †§‡

Y-[_] I will Yield to the Will of God, who has already Clearly Stated in some other Inspired Book that we Tax Slaves MUST Demand **"The Great Worldwide Televised Court Hearing!"** Therefore, it is now Time to get on with it, come next April.

Z-[_] Rest Assured, the Great Zeal of our Selected King will make it Happen in Due Season, whether or not he is Dead or Alive: beCause his Inspired Books of Provable Truths are Eternal Witnesses against all Wicked People, and Testimonies in Favor of the Righteous Ones, who will Love them for their Goodness, and Learn HOW to Divide or Separate the Truths from the Lies.

18-04 [_] O Adolf, if those Lying Edomites do not Want to Cooperate with you and your Selected King, and also Demand that Great Meeting of the Most Intelligent and Well-Educated Minds, we could Organize a Great March on Washington, whereby 60 Million Young People could show up at **"The BIG White OUTHOUSE on the Not-so-Biblical Capitol DUNGHILL!"** (Book 023) and thus let those Politicians Know that we Mean Business! †§‡

18-05 [_] Well, I would say that it would be a HUGE Waste of Time, Energy, Money, and Materials, which would be more Wisely spent in the Construction of **"The Great World TEMPLE of PEACE!"** (Book 017), whereby we might have something to Show for it.

18-06 [_] O Adolf, there must be a Way to Accomplish what is Right and Good for the Masses of People. Why do you not take yourself to the Streets, and Preach your Messages to the Masses of Ignorant People, until they get Inspired?

18-07 [_] Well, I have Thought about it, and several Times, only to Conclude that I would soon be Assassinated by the Hired Thugs of those Lying Edomites: beCause I have made myself an Enemy of practically every Profession in the World, from Washington, District of Chief Criminals, right on down to the Lowest Cockroaches in the City Dumps, who are Addicted to their Drugs. In Fact, I have Thought about giving up on them, and saying: "To Hell with all of them." But, then I am Reminded that if other Brave Spiritual Souls had not made a lot of Sacrifices to Save my Soul, and thus Wrote their Good Books, I would still be Wandering about in the Wilderness of Sins without a Compass, while not knowing where to go for Salvation.

18-08 [_] O Adolf, are you not Educated enough to Know that Salvation is only Found in Jesus Christ, who is the Savior of Mankind, Animalkind and Plantkind, who are Counting on him to Return with Power and Great Glory in the Dark Awesome ROLLING Clouds of a FEARSOME Sky with tens of thousands of his Holy Angels, with a Great Flock of Flying Saucers, whereby the Sky will be Darkened by them? Indeed, he will come from Mount Zion with a Great Army like we have never Seen before, and all of them will be in Perfect Harmony, Dancing in the Sky, and Moving like Lightning! Yes, it will be a FEARFUL Sight to Behold, whereby all Knees will become as Weak as Water, and all People will Fall to the Ground, being TERRIFIED! Therefore, whomever is not HOLY, even as Jesus is Holy, will be most Ashamed: beCause they are not Prepared to Enter into his Holy Kingdom. ‡

18-09 [_] Well, what you say could be True, and if it is True, our Selected King is probably one of the very Few People on the Whole Earth who is at least somewhat Prepared for his Second Coming, while most People are not even Concerned with that Subject.

18-10 [_] O Adolf, just Think of how Wonderful it would be if Jesus Christ would Suddenly Appear at: **"The Great Worldwide TELEVISED Court HEARING!"** Yes, there is a Good Chance that he might Do it, if we Human Beings get everything Ready for him, and Built **"The Great World TEMPLE of PEACE,"** in Jerusalem, where he can Govern this World of Wonders by Means of his New RIGHTEOUS One-World Government!

— Chapter 19 —

Honest White Israelites will Triumph!

19-01 [_] We must Remember that Honest White Israelites are somewhat like Jesus Christ and his Self-disciplined Disciples, who did not have a Greedy Selfish Bone in their Bodies, you might say; or, as Saint Peter said to the Lame Man, who had never Walked: *"Silver and Gold have I none; but, of such Things as I have, I will Give to you, for Free: because I Received them for Free as Gifts from God — in the Name of Jesus Christ of Nazareth of Galilee, rise up and walk."* And then Peter took him by the right Hand, and lifted him up; and immediately his Feet and Ankle Bones received their Strength, and thus he stood up and Walked, and went Leaping and Running and Praising God; and thus all of the People saw him Walking and Praising God, and they knew that it was the Man who had sat at the Beautiful Gate of the Temple, Begging for Alms; and thus they were Filled with Wonder and Amazement at that which had Happened to him. And then the Man who had been Lame, ran over and scooped up Peter and John into his Arms, and Danced with Great Joy, while the Masses of People ran together unto them under the Porch that is called Solomon's Porch, who were Greatly Wondering what was Happening. And when Peter saw it, he Responded to the People, saying: *"You Men of Israel, why do you Marvel at this Miracle? Moreover, why do you Look so Earnestly on us, as though by our own Power or Holiness we had made this Man to Walk, seeing that it was only by the Gift and Power of God? Yes, it was by the Power of the God of Fathers Abraham, Isaac, and Jacob, even the God of our Fathers, who has Glorified his Chosen Son, Jesus, whom you Jews Delivered up to the Chief Bloodthirsty Edomites, and Denied him in the Presence of Pilate, even when he was Determined to let him go Free; but, you Denied the Holy One and the Just One, who had done nothing but Good Deeds for you, and had Taught to you Important Truths that you had never Learned before; and at last you Desired a Murderer to be Granted his Freedom, in place of the Prince of Life, whom you Killed by Exercising your Democracy, whom God has Raised Up from the Dead, whereof we are Witnesses: because we have Seen him and Handled him and Talked with him for many Days, who has Blest us with Special Gifts, which you cannot Rightly Deny: because you have Seen this Man with your own Eyes, who was made Strong by our Faith in Jesus Christ, and by his Faith in Jesus Christ; yes, the Faith, which is by the Gift of Jesus, has given to him this Perfect Soundness of Flesh and Bones in the Presence of all of you. And now, Brothers, I know that through your Ignorance you did a Horrible Thing to the Humble Honest Man from Galilee, as did your Edomite Rulers, also; but, you can be Forgiven, if you Repent: because God has Allowed all of those Evil Things to Happen for our Salvation, in Order to Fulfill the Laws of God, which Demand Justice for All, including Justice for the Original Sin in the Garden of Eden, whereby the First Man, Adam, Ate of the Forbidden Food, whereby Adam and Eve were Cast Out of the Garden of Good Eating, into this World of Woes, whose Descendants are now Living here. Yes, I tell to you the Truth of it — that First Man was Imperfect at that Time; but, behold, he has now been brought to Perfection as the Second Adam, even as the Chosen Son of the Most High God, whereby he Paid the Price for the Original Sin by his Death on the Torture Stake, whereby Justice was Served. Therefore, if we Repent, and Confess all of our Sins, and Believe in him, we can be Saved from all of our Sins, and even Enter into his Holy Kingdom, if we are found Worthy by Reason of our Self-discipline and Righteousness in his Eyes, according to his*

Divine Laws: because he is Able and Willing to Save us. However, if we do not Repent of all of our Sins, and even Attempt to Hide them: because of the Great Shame of them, he cannot Forgive us, nor Cleanse us from all Unrighteousness, even though he Wants to: because that would also be Contrary to the Laws of God, who is a God of True Justice, who will Reward us Justly when we are Born Again, even in a Better World, if we are found to be Worthy of it. Therefore, Repent by Means of Fasting and Praying, and thus be Converted from your Evil Ways: so that your Sins might be Blotted Out, when the Times of Refreshing and Restoration shall come from the Presence of the Supreme Ruler, and he shall Send Jesus Christ to be our Righteous King, whose Kingdom was Preached to all of us by John the Baptist, who came to Prepare the Way for his First Coming, whom the Heaven must Receive until the Times of the Restitution of all Things, which God has Spoken about by the Mouths of all of his Holy Prophets since the World began, which Scriptures were Mutilated by those Lying False Jews, who are Edomites, who Carefully Removed many Key Verses of Scriptures: so that they might Pervert the Scriptures, and set up themselves as Chief Authorities. Nevertheless, we can still read that Moses said to the Fathers in the Wilderness, 'A Holy Prophet shall the Supreme Ruler your God raise up unto you of your Brothers, like me, who shall do many Wonderful Works and Great Miracles; and therefore, him shall you Hear in all Things, whatsoever he shall Command you; and it shall come to pass that every Soul who will not Hear and Obey that Prophet shall be Destroyed from among the People.' Yes, and all of the Holy Prophets from Samuel and onward, as many as have Spoken and Written Words, have likewise Foretold of these Last Days. Yes, some of you are the Children of the Prophets, and of the Covenant, which God made with our Fathers, saying to Abraham, 'And in your Seed shall all of the Kindreds of the Earth be Blest, speaking of Isaac. Therefore, unto you First has God Blest you by Raising Up his Chosen Son, Jesus Christ, and Sent him to Bless us, who have in Turn Blest you by Turning Away everyone of you from your Iniquities, if it so be that you Hear and Obey our Words of Truths. Likewise, it shall come to pass during the Last Day, before the Great and Dreadful Day of the Supreme Ruler comes, that God will Send the Man with the Spirit of Elijah to Correct you, once again: because you will also be Born Again at that Time: because it Requires many Lives for us to Learn all of our Lessons, whereby we must be Tested, again and again, until we are brought to Perfection for either Good or Evil. Therefore, do not Yield to the Temptations of the Devil, who is that Great Deceiver; but, Listen to the Spirit of Truths, and Obey her Voice, whereby you shall Obtain Wisdom and True Nolij." — NMV of a Part of Acts 3.

19-02 [_] O Adolf, why did you not go on with Chapter 4, which Reveals what Happens to People who Teach Reincarnation, whereby People are Resurrected into this World of Wonders, again and again, until we, at Last, Learn our Lessons?

19-03 [_] Well, now that the Key Words have been Restored, you can Understand Chapter 4, whereby you can Magnify it within your own Mind, and thus make Good Sense of it. Otherwise, you should Carefully Read **"The New MAGNIFIED Version of the Book of ACTS!" (The Understandable Version of the ACTS of the Apostles in Plain English!) By The Worldwide People's Revolution!® Book 063.**

19-04 [_] O Adolf, I sure Hope to God that your Selected King gets around to Writing, **"The New MAGNIFIED Version of the PSALMS of King David!" (The Understandable Version of the Famous Psalms in Plain English!)**, Book 064, before he Dies of Old Age!

19-05 [_] Well, that will be in the Hands of God, who Controls the Spirits of all Flesh. Indeed, even if he Dies, he can be Resurrected as a Young Man. (See *Numbers 16:22 and 27:16.*)

19-06 [_] O Adolf, would not all of those Inspired Books have a PRIORITY over all such Uninspired Books as this?

19-07 [_] Well, of what Value would such *Scriptures* be, if the Masses of People are not Persuaded to Study them? Indeed, most People are SPOOKED by the *Scriptures,* and thus they Steer Clear of all such Books. Otherwise, it would be Popular for People to Read the *Scriptures.*

19-08 [_] O Adolf, they Fail to Read the *Scriptures:* beCAUSE the Unholy Mutilated *Bible* cannot be Trusted: beCAUSE it is Full of Contradictions, Confusion, and Barbaric Elizabethan English. †§‡

19-09 [_] Well, that is all the more Reason WHY that our Selected King must write another Inspired Book, called: **"Those Ridiculous Contradictions within the Holy Bible!" (HOW to Read the Unholy Mutilated Bible with an Open Mind!) By The Worldwide People's Revolution!®** Book 057. Yes, the Masses of People must Hear that Confession, and come to Understand that it was Lying Edomites who Mutilated the *Holy Bible,* and made a Big Mess of it, whereby most People do not Understand it, when it should be the most Understandable of all Books: beCause it is supposed to be the Good Instruction Manual for Mankind, which was Inspired by GOD, who is All that is GOOD, who Loves Plainness of Speech, who is NOT the Author of Confusion: beCause SATAN is the Author of Confusion. †§‡

19-10 [_] O Adolf, I still Prefer to Read the Inspired Books of your Selected King! After all, they are far more Educational than the *Old Testament,* and much more Enlightening than the *New Testament,* even though, without those Biblical Books, there would be NO Inspired Books by your Selected King: beCause he was Inspired by them! Therefore, we can only Thank God for the Man with the Spirit of Elijah, who has come to Restore the Great Truths that can set us Free from the Prison of Edomite LIES, whereby they have made Education Slaves, Work Slaves, Tax Slaves, Interest Slaves, Insurance Slaves, Drug Slaves, Sex Slaves, Debt Slaves, Rent Slaves, ElecTrickery Bills Slaves, Gas Bills Slaves, Water Bills Slaves, Entertainment Bills Slaves, Transportation Bills Slaves, and Endless Bills Slaves of us Deceived Capitalists. †§‡

(HOW to be Liberated from all Slavery, Worldwide!)

— Chapter 20 —

The Conclusion

20-01 [_] As "Painful" as it might seem to be, there is only One Way Out of the Prison of Lies that we are now Locked Up in, and that is to pass Through the Doorway of Confession, which Confession must Begin with those Lying Edomites, who Control the Big Banks and the Money Supplies, whereby they are the "Puppet Masters," who Control the Strings of Politicians, News Reporters, Book Publishers, Hollywood Movies, and the General Propaganda Machine, whereby the Masses of People Sincerely Believe that they are the "Good Guys," when, in Fact, they are of the Synagogue of Satan, just Exactly as Jesus Christ Identified them, which can now be Proven at: **"The Great Worldwide TELEVISED Court HEARING!" (That Great Meeting of the Most Intelligent and Well-Educated Minds!) By The Worldwide People's Revolution!®** Book 041. Indeed, it is now Time to Serve Justice to all of them, and Rebuild those Nazi Crematory Ovens, if they do not Cheerfully Agree to DEMAND and Attend that Great Meeting, whereby the Whole Truth might be Discovered about all Kinds of Important Subjects, and the Education Slaves, Work Slaves, Tax Slaves, Interest Slaves, Debt Slaves, Insurance Slaves, Sex Slaves, Childcare Slaves, ElecTrickery Bills Slaves, Transportation Slaves, and Endless Bills Slaves might be Set FREE! †§‡

20-02 [_] O Adolf, I must Agree with you — that it is High Time for us to Discover the Whole Truth; but, to Rebuild those Nazi Ovens seems to be a bit Radical to me. Are you Suggesting that we will have to Build Nazi Concentration Camps, and Round Up all Edomites, and Roast them Thoroughly? †§‡

20-03 [_] NO! I am not saying any such Evil Thing: beCause X-amount of Edomites are Actually Honest White Jews, who have been Misnamed, who will be the FIRST to See the Light, and DEMAND that Great Meeting of the Most Intelligent Minds: beCause they have nothing to Fear: because they have done nothing WRong. Indeed, they will LOVE the Justice of it all. Therefore, if you know of any Jews or Edomites of any Kind, PLEASE do your Best to get a Copy of this Inspired Book into their Hands: beCause it will Greatly Help to Heat Up the Great Cauldron that Separates the Meat from the Scum, and thus get the Political Stew Brewing. †‡

20-04 [_] O Adolf, you are likely to be Arrested and Sentenced to Prison for Inciting Racial Riots, and Promoting Anti-Semitic Propaganda, etc., etc., even though I Believe that you have Good Intentions, and only Seek True Justice. Could you not just Cool it, and put up with the Education Slavery, Work Slavery, Tax Slavery, Interest Slavery, Debt Slavery, Sex Slavery, Drug Slavery, Insurance Slavery, and Endless Bills Slavery, seeing that you have already Retired without any Unsociable Insecurity Check? Indeed, why bring down the Evil Empires for the Sakes of Billions of Ignorant Goyim, who will never know the Difference, if you do not Tell them HOW they could all be Living in **"Beautiful Swanky PALACES!" (A New Concept in Living Habits — Swanky Palaces for Poor People!) By The Worldwide People's Revolution!®**, Book 066?

20-05 [_] Well, I would rather Suffer Persecutions, and even be Crucified with Jesus Christ, rather than go to Hell with a Bad Conscience, in Order to Try to Justify the Evil Works of Lying Edomites, who have Managed to make SLAVES of almost everyone in the Whole World. After all, the Tax Slaves are NOT of a Lower Order than those Lying Edomites, who are not one Degree Better than any of the Remainder of us People, even as I am not one Degree Better than anyone else, except by the Grace of God! ‡

20-06 [_] O Adolf, are you saying that you ARE Better than the Remainder of us: beCause of the Grace of God, even as King David was Better than King Saul by the Grace of God?

20-07 [_] Well, my Friend, you will have to Confess, sooner or later, that we were not all Born Equal in all Ways. In Fact, none of us were Born Equal with anyone in any Way: beCause we are all Different in many Ways, and some of us are more Righteous than others; but, only by the Grace of God: beCause we did not make ourselves Righteous, except by the Grace of God, who Helped us through the Inspired Words of Jesus Christ and other Holy Ones to make ourselves more Righteous. Therefore, we can only Thank God for Jesus Christ and his Inspired Words of Provable Truths, including those of our Selected King, who was Inspired by Jesus and others. ‡

20-08 [_] O Adolf, it Appears to me that whomever Controls the Propaganda Machine also Controls whatever most People Believe, which is WHY we have Freedom of Speech and Freedom of the Press, whereby all Voices might be Heard, just in case some of those Voices might be Revealing Truths that we all Need to Learn, just to keep our Minds Well Balanced, and thus not become Radical Fanatics like Adolf Hitler, who Vainly Imagined that the Germans could Take Over the Whole World by FORCE of Military Arms! †§‡

20-09 [_] Well, I am now here to Inform you that Adolf Hitler had no such Evil Intentions, nor did he ever Mention any such Silly Things in any of his Speeches. Therefore, you should Stop Preaching all such False Doctrines about Adolf Hitler, who was only Seeking Justices for the Germans, which is WHY the Germans Loved him so much, and were thus Willing to DIE for the Cause, and with Great Enthusiasm, which is WHY it Required the entire Capitalist and Communist Worlds to Defeat those Determined Germans, who had very Limited Resources to Work with, while the Capitalists and Communists had 95% of the Natural Resources to Work with, which made it an Unfair War Game, you might say. Indeed, it would be like 5 Men without Sufficient Ammunition Attempting to Conquer 95 Men who are Well Equipped. Therefore, we must Admire the Germans for their Heroic Struggle for Justice, even as we have to Admire the South for their Heroic Struggle during the Great Civil War, who were Attempting to Defeat the North, which had a hundred Times more Resources of Men, Equipment and Natural Resources to Work with, which was another Unfair War Game — except that the North had a more Righteous Cause to be Fighting for in the Eyes of most People, without Understanding that the South was Fighting for the Constitution and States Rights, which was Justified in their Eyes, which is WHY that they also Fought with such Great Enthusiasm, while the North could not even Understand WHY they were Fighting, except to Liberate some Black Slaves, who are now Locked Up in Prisons all of the Country, who are in Worse Conditions than their Fathers and Mothers. †§‡

20-10 [_] O Adolf, all such Arguments could go on and on for ever and ever without the Light of Enlightenment. {See: **"All of the Arguments are in Favor of our Selected King, who has Zero Challengers!" (Before you Attend another Election Deception, you should Study this Inspired Book with an Open Mind!) By The Worldwide People's Revolution!® Book 085.**}

(HOW to be Liberated from all Slavery, Worldwide!)

— Chapter 21 —

— The Appendix —

An E-mail Letter to Saint John McArdle of C-SPAN Fame

21-01 [_] Monday, June 27th, 2016 — another Day in Infamy!

21-02 [_] Brother John,

21-03 [_] Thank you for your Programs this morning on the *Washington Journal.* You are so Beautiful! Such a Good Heart and Mind! We cannot help but Love you for what you are and what you have been doing! Keep up the Good Work!

21-04 [_] To Answer your very Important Question about how common it is for Illegal Immigrants to own and operate Businesses in the United States, while hiding under the "Radar," (in "Secret") without being detected by the Authorities? — you will do well to consider WHO Gains more Wealth by all such Houses and Businesses, which often go Out of Business: beCause those Poor Illegal Immigrants have most often visited their local "Friendly Bankers," who have "Kindly" encouraged them to Borrow Money for Buying Houses and Businesses, whereby they become "Eternal" Interest Slaves of the Friendly Bankers, who are Laughing at them all of the way into their Bank Vaults: because, after getting all such Interest Slaves in the "Right Positions," being the Proud "OWNERS" of 2 or 3 or more Wooden / Plastic Firetrap Mouse-infested Cockroach Dens, and possibly some similar Businesses, also, after 20+ Years of Slave Labor for the entire Family, "it is time to get them deported," thinks the Benevolent Banker, which only requires a simple Telephone Call to ICE (Illegal Coldhearted ENFORCEMENT agency), whereby those Banksters collect all of their Houses and Businesses, and possibly their Vehicles, Furniture, and Land, also: because the Deported Victims of Capitalism are Unable to Pay their Usury, whereby those Friendly Bankers REPOSSESS all such Properties, Legally. ‡

21-05 [_] Yes, that is the Customary Practice of many Unethical Bankers, which can be, should be and must be Proven in a Courtroom, which Atrocious Acts are all Legal in America, which the Lawyers also know about: beCause they are a Part of the Conspiracy against those Poor Ignorant Illegal Immigrants, who handle the Property Deeds for them, who are also only interested in getting their Money, who are often Club Members with those Friendly Bankers, who know exactly what they are doing! ‡

21-06 [_] And now it is Time for you, Dear Brother John McArdle, to Learn what they are doing "Under the Radar," in Secret, in "The Greatest Nation on the Earth!" Trust me, there is no Law against what those Bankers and Lawyers are doing. Moreover, you may now Judge for yourself whether or not you are now Living in "The Most WICKED Nation on the Earth," as some of those "Radical Muslims" claim, who are not nearly so Ignorant nor Stupid as many Americans! Indeed, they are Aware of what is going on: because similar Evil Things have Happened to them, which have been Reported among them, whereby they are Aware of the TRUTH; but, not the Whole Truth, or else they might Discover HOW to Overthrow the Evil Empire without Firing a single Shot! ‡

21-07 [_] The Federal Burden of Investigation (FBI), under the Direction of James Comey, is also Aware of that Conspiracy against those Poor Ignorant Illegal Immigrants, who number in the tens of millions, most of whom have "Bought" Houses, and never got to Actually OWN such Houses without the "Services" of those "Friendly Banksters." But, not to Worry: because NONE of the CONgress People are Aware of it: because they are all Ignorant Innocent Americans, much like you and I used to be, Brother John — even the "Good Guys," whom not even you will Inform about it: beCause you have no Way to even Contact them, right? I certainly do not. They have no E-mail Addresses for the General Public to Write anything to them. §

21-08 [_] Nevertheless, if you have any Love, Empathy, or Compassion for those Poor Illegal Immigrants, you might discover some way to Forward this E-mail Letter to ALL of those Congress People, the President, the Supreme Court "Justices," and the Pastors, Priests, Preachers, Professors, Doctors, Lawyers, Teachers, and Authors of Books — just by Means of a Click or 2 on your Computer Screen: beCause, you Live in "The Greatest Nation on the Earth," which does not even have a Way to Distribute any such Provable Truths: beCause the News Media is Controlled by the Chief Banksters, who would never Allow such Information to get into the NEWS: beCause Edomite Bankers are our PETS, whom we must not Offend at all Costs. ‡

21-09 [_] Yes, if you Doubt it, just Ask those Friendly CONgress People, who are Puppets on their Strings, who could easily Pass a Bill in Congress, stating that: "NO BANKER may Loan ANY Money to ANY Illegal Immigrant, lest he or she should be Deported to the nearest Federal Prison, and be put to Work at Hard Labor on Minimum Rations of Beans, Turnips, Hot Bitter Green Onions, Garlic and Rancid Peanuts, with only Recycled Sewage Water to Drink, which has been Recycled from the Toilet Drains of State Capitals." Otherwise, those Greedy Edomite Bankers could be Beheaded with **"The Swanky Sword of Divine Truths!"** Book 067.

21-10 [_] And now, Big-hearted Brother John, you can Understand with a Capital U, how easy it is for "LEGAL" Immigrants to "Fall into the same Pit," by Overstaying their Visas, whereby they also Visit those Friendly Bankers, and get into the same Deep Dark PIT as Interest Slaves for Houses that they seldom Actually "OWN." However, even if they did Actually Own them, they would still be what those "Radical Muslims" call: "Education Slaves, Work Slaves, Tax Slaves, Insurance Slaves, Interest Slaves, and Endless Bills Slaves," who would be Repeatedly "Re-Buying" such "Good Houses," by Means of "Property Taxes, Theft Insurance Bills, Repair Bills, Renovations, Refurbishing, Upgrades, Carpet Replacements, Lead Water Pipe Replacements, Heating and Cooling Bills, Gas Bills, ElecTRICKERY Bills, Water Bills, Fire Insurance Bills, Tornado Insurance Bills, Flood-damage Insurance Bills, Hail Insurance Bills, etc., etc.!" — which you surely know about! ‡

21-11 [_] But, if you are Unaware of the Evils of Capitalism, just Watch the latest Snooze Reports, and Listen to the Pleading Voices of those Pitiful Callers on the *Washington Journal,* on

(HOW to be Liberated from all Slavery, Worldwide!)

the C-SPAN Network, on whom you have had NO Mercy by Directing them to our Selected King, who has **"Guaranteed Solutions!" (HOW to Solve our Local and Global Problems in the Most Rational Manner Possible!) By The Worldwide People's Revolution!®** Book 080.

21-12 [_] Sincerely, The Chief Agitator

21-13 [_] PS — This Letter is COPYRIGHTED 2016 by The Chief Agitator, which will also be Forwarded to our Selected King, and to: The Leader, Adolf Dictator Hitler, Junior! Be Aware of it. All Rights are Reserved for the Federal Burden of Investigation, and the Central Unintelligent Agencies, who have yet to Discover those Most Enlightening Books by our Selected King, which present Real Workable Guaranteed Solutions!

21-14 [_] O Adolf, why would you Contaminate such a Good Book as this by Inserting a Nasty Anti-American Appendix along the "WRECKtum" of it, which Stinks with Legalistic Neo-NAZI Nonsense: because there is no Way on this Good Earth that all such Sarcastic Commentaries will ever be Printed nor Published by Lying Edomites, who Control the Book Publishing Companies, who only want to Sell GOOD Books — such as "The Best Democratic Government that Money Can Buy!" †§‡§§

21-15 [_] Well, X-amount of those Book Publishing Companies are Controlled by Honest White Israelites, who Believe in all such Provable Truths, who are not at all Ashamed to Publish such Things: because they Know for a Fact that the Truth will Win in the Battle of Controversial Thoughts, such as are Presented above for all Thinking Sober-minded People. After all, anyone could be Born in some Poor Foreign Country the next Time Around, and thus have to Experience what it is Like to be a Mistreated Alien, Refugee, Migrant Worker, Illegal Immigrant, Abused Tax Slave, or whatever: because we have all of Eternity to Learn all such Good Lessons. ‡ {See www.Amazon.com for: **"AIIRMWVC!" (Aliens, Illegal Immigrants, Refugees, Migrant Workers and other Victims of Capitalism!) By The Worldwide People's Revolution!®** Book 032.}

21-16 [_] O Adolf, if this Format is Open Phone Lines again on the *Washington Journal,* I would like your Permission to make another Comment, if you do not Object?

21-17 [_] Well, go ahead, and make your Comment, since there is still some Space on the Page to make it.

21-18 [_] O Adolf, it is my Honest Opinion that the Reason WHY the United States Federal Government does not Invest much Money in Infrastructure Projects — such as Repairing Highways, Bridges, Sewage Systems, and the Electric Grid — is beCAUSE they are already Aware that **"GLORIOUS Swanky Hotels Castles and Fortresses"** have no less than 5,000 Advantages over normal Cities of Confusion; and therefore, they do not want to Waste any Hard-earned Tax Money, Materials, nor Energy on all such Vain Projects, which will eventually be Abandoned, anyway. What do you Think? †

21-19 [_] Well, if they do know about those Beautiful Planned City States for Wise Intelligent Well-Educated People with Common Sense and Good Understanding, Book 019, it is for Sure that they are keeping it a Big Secret: because I have never Heard them make any Mention of them, have you? Therefore, that is Evidence that they have not Studied any such Exceptionally Good Books: because no one with a Sound Honest Mind could Ignore all such Provable Truths. Otherwise, if they have Studied all such Exceptionally Good Books, they are Deliberately Hiding the Information unto their own Great Shame when it is Revealed at: **"The Great Worldwide TELEVISED Court HEARING!" (That Great Meeting of the Most Intelligent and Well-Educated Minds! By The Worldwide People's Revolution!® Book 041.**

21-20 [_] O Adolf, they do not Want the Masses of People to Learn that they know anything about those Planned Cities: beCause, if the Education Slaves, Work Slaves, Tax Slaves, Interest Slaves, Insurance Slaves, and Endless Bills Slaves should ever Discover that they have known about those Beautiful Planned City States for no less than 30 Years, those Slaves would never Forgive them for Keeping it a Top Secret! Indeed, those Slaves would likely Hang all of them High on Electric Light Posts. †

21-21 [_] Well, that is Debatable, seeing that most Americans are too Lazy to even Read a Good Book, much less Hoist anyone up to a Light on a Post, which would require much more Energy.

21-22 [_] O Adolf, it is not beCause Americans are too Lazy to read a Book; but, it is only beCause they have not yet HEARD about your Exceptionally Good Books. Therefore, it is the Duty of the Readers to Encourage their Friends, Relatives, Naaberz, and even their Enemies, to read all such Inspired Books — if only to leave such Books lying on the Sidewalks, Bus Seats, Subway Train Seats, or wherever other People might Discover them, by Chance. After all, one of the Best Books that I have ever read was Discovered by Chance on a Bus Seat in a Busy City of Confusion.

21-23 [_] Well, that is a Good Idea; but, only IF you can Afford to Distribute such Books as this one, which Costs 10$, which you could possibly get Printed up for 4$, and Sell them for 7$ on the Streets, IF you got a large Volume of them Printed at one Time, and only IF you Discovered that such Books Sell well enough to make it Worth the Investment, and only IF you had Sufficient Money for making such an Investment?

21-24 [_] O Adolf, the Title of this Book is not very Attractive to most Americans, who would be Afraid to Sell such a Book on the Streets: because it seems to be Anti-Semitic, which might even land some of them in Jail for a Day or 2, just for that Reason. However, our Selected King has many Attractive Titles on other Inspired Books, which can be found in Verse 09-03, which would not be "Dangerous" to Publish on the Streets. In Fact, they would make a really Great Book Display in any Book Store, and a Better Display on any Street, if some Congregation of Believers can Muster Up the Faith, Hope, Trust, Love, Patience, Persistence and OBEDIENCE to Do that by United Effort! {See www.Amazon.com for: **"The Seven Basic Spiritual Building Blocks of LIFE!" Book 036.**}

21-25 [_] I Agree with you — that there are much Better Books in the Swanky TRUTH-brary — but, this is a more Controversial Book, which might become a "Best Seller" on certain Streets, even on Wall Street, in New York City, where it might Stir Up the Lions and Wolves. Therefore, if someone is a very Brave Soul, and wants to get some ACTION, that is a Good Place to Set Up and Sell a few Exceptionally Good Books — such as those that Deal with Construction and **"The New RIGHTEOUS One-World Government"**; but, only with PERMISSION: because it is

Doubtful that there is any True Freedom of Speech and Press in **"The Divided States of United Lies,"** which you can Prove by Attempting to Sell such a Controversial Book as this!

21-26 [_] O Adolf, I Promise to give it a Test. Moreover, I will Check the Box, and Sign my Name below for a Witness at: **"The Great Worldwide TELEVISED Court HEARING!"** Book 041. Yes, that little Check Mark (X) with Red Ink, and my Signature below my Printed Name, could possibly "Earn" a Good Position for me in your New RIGHTEOUS One-World GovernMINT!

— Chapter 22 —

A so-called "Long Boring List" of other Fascinating Literature by the same Inspired Author!

[_] 22-01 — **"LIGHTNING Versus the Lightning Bug!"** (HOW almost Everyone can become Moderately RICH, without Telling Any Lies nor Selling Any Trash!) Book 001.

[_] 22-02 — **"What is WRong with those Professing Christians?"** (A Self-Examination of the Heart of the Body of Good Government!) Book 002.

[_] 22-03 — **"For the Love of Money!"** (The Strange Things that People Say and Do to Get more Money!) Book 003.

[_] 22-04 — **"HOW to Prepare for CLIMATE CHANGES!"** (The Wisest Plan for Mankind to Follow!) Book 004.

[_] 22-05 — **"Why do I have to be Surrounded by CRAZY PEOPLE!"** (Do almost all People Feel like they are Surrounded by CRAZY People??) Book 005.

[_] 22-06 — **"The Washington Journal is a FARCE! (C-SPAN Managers are not very WISE!)** Book 006. (This Book has lots of Good Humor.)

[_] 22-07 — **"The PRAYERS of PUMPKINHEADS!"** (Even God Needs a Little Humor to Cheer himself Up!) Book 007. (Some of it is for Adults only.)

[_] 22-08 — **"A Sound Argument for Masters and Servants!"** (WHY Everyone Needs a Good Master, and every Master Needs Good Obedient Servants!) Book 008.

[_] 22-09 — **"WHY are some Preachers so POOR?"** (HOW almost all Preachers could Get Moderately RICH, without Preaching any Outlandish LIES!) Book 009.

[_] 22-10 — **"GOOD NEWS for REBEL WOMEN!"** (HOW almost all Wives can become Moderately RICH without Leaving their Homes! Guaranteed!) Book 010.

[_] 22-11 — **"The Low Court of Supreme Injustices is Brought to Trial!"** (The Worldwide People's Revolution!® Butts Heads with the United States Supreme Court, with or without their Black Robes of Hypocrisies and Lies!) Book 011. (This Inspired Book contains the Famous *Declaration of Interdependence,* which is a Must Read. It also contains the Correct Wording for the Placard on the Statue of Liberty.)

[_] 22-12 — **"The Right Design for Living!"** (A List of Great Advantages for Building Beautiful Planned City States!) Book 012. (This Book contains many Important Drawings, as well as HOW to Save hundreds of Trillions of Dollars by Building Swanky Fortresses, and Living in Peace within them. It is a Companion Book of Book 011, which contains many more Great Advantages for Fortresses.)

[_] 22-13 — **"The Gospel According to The Worldwide People's Revolution!®"** (The Good News from the Most Modern Perspective!) Book 013. (This Book contains the Famous Sermon of Jonah to the Ninevites, whereby 120,000 People Repented in Sackcloth and Ashes! Do not Miss Out on it.)

[_] 22-14 — **"Poverty Hunger Riots Strikes Brutalities Election Deceptions and Civil Wars!"** (The High Price that we Earthlings have Paid for Leaving the Good Land!) Book 014.

[_] 22-15 — **"Seven Great Armies of Working Soldiers!"** (HOW to Provide a Way for Everyone to WORK: so as to Eliminate Poverty, Crimes, Drug Abuses, Prisons and Unnecessary Taxes!) Book 015. (This Book contains a True Life Story when I was in the Army.)

[_] 22-16 — **"The CONSTITUTION for the New RIGHTEOUS One-World GovernMint!"** (HOW all Peoples can get True Justice, and Celebrate the Great Year of JUBILEE!) Book 016.

[_] 22-17 — **"The Great World TEMPLE of PEACE!"** (The Glory of Jerusalem Arises Again!) By The Worldwide People's Revolution!® Book 017.

[_] 22-18 — **"The Swanky Associations of Working Soldiers!"** (A Fascinating Collection of Various Kinds of Voluntary Working Soldiers!) Book 018. (There will be thousands of Associations for all Kinds of Occupations, which will Specialize in Fine Arts — such as Hand-carved Leather-bound Books. See **"LIGHTNING STRIKES Versus Lightning Bugs!"** Book 074, for a Good Example.)

[_] 22-19 — **"GLORIOUS Swanky Hotels Castles and Fortresses!"** (Beautiful Planned City States for WISE Intelligent Well-Educated People with Common Sense and Good Understanding!) Book 019. (This Book contains many Rough Drawings, which could be Greatly Improved upon by someone who Knows the Art, and has the Correct Computer Programs for doing it.)

[_] 22-20 — **"Are you a Jobless Graduate of the SKQL uv FQLZ?"** (HOW to Get a GOUD EJUKAASHUN without Robbing the Bank!) Book 020. (This Inspired Book contains the

(HOW to be Liberated from all Slavery, Worldwide!)

New MAGNIFIED Version {NMV} of *First Corinthians 13,* plus: HOW to Produce Pure Living Water!)

[_] 22-21 — **"The LUSCIOUS All-Mineral Organic Method of Gardening!"** (**HOW to Grow DELICIOUS Satisfying Foods for Potential Kingz and Kweenz in Beautiful Swanky PALACES!)** Book 021. (This Book Explains HOW to make a Flood-proof Garden, while Trapping the Rainwater.)

[_] 22-22 — **"Did God or Satan Ordain Medical Doctors?"** (**Ask Huck Finn and/or Nigger Jim: because neither Tom Sawyer nor Judge Thatcher would Know!)** Book 022. (This Inspired Book Reveals HOW to Prevent Common Colds, and has a Special Chapter that Explains what a True "Nigger" IS. Surprise yourself!)

[_] 22-23 — **"The BIG White OUTHOUSE on the Not-so-Biblical Capitol DUNGHILL!"** **(The Chief Sins of the Divided States of United Lies!) By The Worldwide People's Revolution!®** Book 023. (This Book contains Special Words that most People have never Heard! Surprise yourself again!)

[_] 22-24 — **"The Public School of IGNERUNT FQLZ!"** (**HOW we have been GRAATLEE DISEEVD by Capitalism!)** Book 024. (This Book Teaches Children HOW to "Reed and Riit in Funetik Ingglish in just wun Daa!" You should Challenge your Frendz and Naaberz with it.)

[_] 22-25 — **"In thu Beeginingz uv Thingz!"** (**Thu Kreeaashun Stooree frum thu Beegining!)** Book 025. {The Cover Photo shows a Picture of a Golden Supootaa (Sapote), which not one Person in a Million has ever Tasted: because it does not Ship very well, in spite of it being one of the most Sweetest Pleasant Fruits known to Mankind, which must Ripen on the Tree to be Extremely Good, after it is Grown Properly by **"The LUSCIOUS All-Mineral Organic Method of Gardening!"** Book 021, which Means that the Topsoil must have all of the Proper Minerals in it. Remember the Grapes of Eschol, which the Children of Israel brought back from the Promised Land in the *Book of Joshua,* which Required 2 Strong Men to Carry just one Cluster! See the Fascinating Photos in: **"Orgimmick Gardening at its Best!"** (**HOW to Grow Delicious Satisfying Foods without a 10-Million-Dollar Investment!) By The Worldwide People's Revolution!®** Book 079.}

[_] 22-26 — **"God Speaks and the Whole World Listens!"** (**Fire on the Mountain from the Burning Bush by the Spirit of Truths!)** Book 026. (This Powerful Book contains the Best Noah Story of all of the Books, including that of Gilgamesh the Great of Ancient Babylon!)

[_] 22-27 — **"Does a Good Soldier have to be a MURDERER?"** (**Seven Great Swanky Armies of Voluntary Working Soldiers!) By The Worldwide People's Revolution!®** Book 027. (Chapter 03 contains a True Life Story about a Dog Pile, which happened to me when I was just 10 Years Old.)

[_] 22-28 — **"Thu Nq MAGNUFIID Verzhun uv Thu PROVERBZ uv KING SOLUMUN in Plaan Ingglish!"** (**The Understandable Version of the Famous Proverbs of King Solomon in Plain English!)** Book 028. (This Marvelous Book MAGNIFIES each Proverb unto the Glory of the Great God of Inspiration, which is taken from the Original 4,000-page Book, which was written in less than 2 Months by the GIFT of Inspiration, which also contains the Famous Proverbs of Queen Izubelu!)

[_] 22-29 — **"UNLIMITED ENERJEE 99 Percent Pollutions Free!"** (HOW to Obtain FREE ElecTrickery, Worldwide!) By The Worldwide People's Revolution!® Book 029. (This Book contains the Jackson Brower Suicide, among many other Fascinating Subjects.)

[_] 22-30 — **"FREEDUM uv SPEECH!"** (U Speshoul Maguzeen uv Onist Upinyunz!) Book 030-0001, which contains the Great Advantages for Using Swanky Mulching Rocks in an All-Mineral Organic Garden, plus Baptism by Fire and Speaking in Foreign Languages! It is a Must Read. The Cover Photo shows a Portion of the Author's Marbleous Indian Countertop or Food Bar, which is just one Example of what you can also have in your own **"Beautiful Swanky PALACES!"** if you have the Honesty, Faith, Hope, Trust, Love, Patience, Persistence, Cooperation and OBEDIENCE that are Required for True Prosperity! Therefore, Ejukaat yourself, and you will be Glad that you did!

[_] 22-31 — **"A Sure Cure for GUN VIOLENCE!"** (HOW TO STOP GANG WARS and CRIMINAL SHOOTINGS!) By The Worldwide People's Revolution!® Book 031. {The Cover Photo shows a Picture of a Short Shotgun, which is Fully Loaded with Double 00 Shells, and is Ready for any Tax Master who might Attempt to Steal the Retirement Home, who never moved a Finger to Help Build the Rock Houses, whereby we moved more than 66,666,666 Pounds by Hand, whose Property was Cunningly Stolen by that False Anti-Christ WICKED Cover-up Government, which allowed Bankers to Rob us of 30 Years of Hard Labor and more than 300,000 dollars-worth of Investments in our Uncommon American Farm, which is Explained in: **"LIGHTNING STRIKES Versus Lightning Bugs!"** (HOW you can Become Moderately RICH, without Telling any Lies nor Selling any Trash!) By The Worldwide People's Revolution!® Book 074, which contains many Photographs with Profound Explanations! Do not be left out in the Darkness of Ignorance. Get Informed, now: beCause, **"The Great False Economy is now DEBUNKED!"** Book 053.}

[_] 22-32 — **"AIIRMWVC and Reasonable Solutions!"** (Aliens, Illegal Immigrants, Refugees, Migrant Workers and other Victims of Capitalism!) By The Worldwide People's Revolution!® Book 032. (This Inspired Book contains *the New MAGNIFIED Version of Job 33.*)

[_] 22-33 — **"Mark Twain Races for the PRESIDENCY!"** (The 2020 Presidential Candidates Desperately Need Some STRONG Undefeatable COMPETITION!) By The Worldwide People's Revolution!® Book 033. {This Book contains a Part of my Autobiography, and my Personal Answers to the Questions in **"The Complete SURVEYS of our VALUES!"** (SURVEYS of Religious Spiritual Political Governmental Sexual Social Moral Economic Business Labor Habitual and Miscellaneous VALUES!) Book 059. It also contains many Black and White Photographs.}

[_] 22-34 — **"ECCLESIASTES UNCOVERED!"** (The New MAGNIFIED Version of Ecclesiastes and the Song of Solomon in Plain English!) Book 034. (This is the Book that

(HOW to be Liberated from all Slavery, Worldwide!)

contains the Famous Sayings for *"There is a Time to be Born, and a Time to Die ..."* which has been Greatly Magnified!)

[_] 22-35 — **"The Environmentalists' Paradise!"** (HOW almost Everyone could be Living in a Beautiful Manmade Paradise!) By The Worldwide People's Revolution!® Book 035. (This Book contains the NMV of *Psalm 48,* which will Amaze you, O Lady Doubtfulness!)

[_] 22-36 — **"The Seven Basic Spiritual Building Blocks of LIFE!"** (Faith Hope Trust Love Patience Persistence and Obedience!) Book 036. (This Book contains the Mockingbird's Version of *Hebrews 11,* plus the NMV of *First Corinthians 13,* among many other "Goodies.")

[_] 22-37 — **"DIETS!"** (A Reasonable Solution for the "Eternal Controversy"!) By The Worldwide People's Revolution!® Book 037.

[_] 22-38 — **"The Nature of CAPITALISM!"** (A List of the EVILS of CAPITALISM!) Book 038.

[_] 22-39 — **"SWANGKEENOMIKS Rules the Roost!"** (HOW all People can Prosper in a RIIT WAA, and STOP Polluting the Earth with Capitalist TRASH!) By The Worldwide People's Revolution!® Book 039. (The Cover Photo shows a Portion of our Retirement Home, before the 5,000+ square-feet Concrete Roof was Installed, after moving more than 66 Million Pounds by Hand!)

[_] 22-40 — **"The New MAGNIFIED Version of The Book of MOORMUN!"** (The Story of the White and Dark Indians in the Americas!) Book 040, which comes in 2 Volumes of about 500 Pages, each. The Cover Photo on the First Volume shows the Queen of England's Golden Coach, and the Cover Photo on the Second Volume shows one of many Polished Spanish Marble Walls in our Retirement Home, which is worth a thousand dollars per square yard, which is another Example of what you can also have, if you simply OBEY your Righteous KING! All such Marble is very Inspiring. No one could Study it for very long without Believing in a Great Creator God. The Picture does not do it Justice. You would have to See it in Person, and Wash it with Pure Water to bring Out the Beauty.

[_] 22-41 — **"The Great Worldwide TELEVISED Court HEARING!"** (That Great Meeting of the Most Intelligent and Wel-Ejukaatid Miindz!) By The Worldwide People's Revolution!® Book 041. {This is the Book that the World has long been Waiting for: beCause it will Overthrow the Evil Empires, and make it Possible to Establish **"The New RIGHTEOUS One-World Government!"** (HOW to Establish a Righteous One-World Government without Going to WAR!) By The Worldwide People's Revolution!® Book 056. This is the Greatest Idea since the Invention of the Light Bulb, Guaranteed!}

[_] 22-42 — **"The Secret City of the Great King!"** (HOW the True Church will Escape from the Great Tribulation!) By The Worldwide People's Revolution!® Book 042. (Be Sure to Inform your Friends, Relatives and Naaberz about this Wonderful Book: beCause they might also Want to Escape!)

[ ] 22-43 — "**Terrorists Beware that your Days are Numbered!**" (HOW to Bring those Terrorist Attacks to a Screeching HALT!) By The Worldwide People's Revolution!® Book 043. (This Book also contains the Fascinating Book of LEHI, which has now been Restored!) †‡

[ ] 22-44 — "**The New MAGNIFIED Version of ISAIAH in Plain English!**" (The Understandable Version of the Book of Isaiah!) Book 044. (The Cover Photo shows a Swanky Potato and Avocado Salad with Sweet Peas and Corn, among other "Secret" Ingredients, which are Revealed within the Book. Remember that you can read many Words for Free in the Book Previews on Amazon.com.usa.)

[ ] 22-45 — "**HOW to Become a HOLY Man!**" (40 Good Reasons WHY People Should FAST and PRAY!) Book 045, which is a Companion Book of:

[ ] 22-46 — "**The Proper RULES for FASTING!**" (The Complete Instruction Manual for True Repentance!) By The Worldwide People's Revolution!® Book 046, which is a Companion Book of the above mentioned Book, which contains a True Life Story about an Old Black Mare called Lucy, who Fasted for 30 Days without Food nor Water, who was Physiologically "Born Again," as Jesus might say. See the Full Details in: "**The New MAGNIFIED Version of The GOOD NEWS According to Saint JOHN!**" (The Gospel According to Saint John Zebedee Boanerges in Plain English!) Book 062, which contains many Inspiring Photographs with Explanations!

[ ] 22-47 — "**Are Americans the Most STUPID People who ever Lived?**" (HOW Working People can PROSPER and Live in PEACE Under the Rulership of a RIGHTEOUS KING!) By The Worldwide People's Revolution!® Book 047. (The Cover Photo shows a large Portion of the Author's Living Room Floor, which is worth 100,000$, which is just another Good Example of what you can also have, just for Loving and Obeying your Elected King!)

[ ] 22-48 — "**An Amazing Collection of Wit and Wisdom!**" (The Marvelous Tale of the Colorful Peacock from Angel Ridge, and the Strong Rope of Everlasting Hope!) By The Worldwide People's Revolution!® Book 048. (The Cover Photo shows a Book Display, which will be Greatly Enhanced during the Future, when all 350+ Inspired Books are on Display in a Swanky Truth-brary, as Opposed to the Public LIE-brary.)

[ ] 22-49 — "**Justifications for Capitalizations!**" (WHY The Worldwide People's Revolution!® Defies the School of Fools by Capitalizing LOVE and HATE!) Book 049.

[ ] 22-50 — "**The END of CONFUSION!**" (The Great CELEBRATION of the Magnificent Wedding of the Most Humble Honest Nations, and the Grand Year of JUBILEE!) By The Worldwide People's Revolution!® Book 050. (Just Try to Visualize those "**Seven Great Swanky Armies of Voluntary Working Soldiers**" Marching through the Valley of Megiddo, being Dressed in their Colorful Robes, while the Band Plays *The Battle Hymn of the Republic,* and the Choirs Sing the Praises of the Great KING of Kings! What a Sight and Sound that will be, which will be Climaxed in "**The Great World TEMPLE of PEACE,**" when the Nations will get Married, along with our Elected King! Come one, come all to "**The Great Worldwide TELEVISED Court HEARING,**" by Means of your Wide Flat-screen TVs, whereby you might Learn WHY, WHEN and HOW!) †‡

[_] 22-51 — **"The Loathsome Burdens of the Independent Jackasses!" (A New Approach for Solving our Massive Problems!) By The Worldwide People's Revolution!® Book 051.** (Just Think about the Multitude of almost Worthless Meetings of the Minds, who Strained themselves to Think of Reasonable Solutions for our Massive Problems, who sometimes even Prayed to God for Help; but, the Solutions have been here for no less than 40 Years — Thanks to the Spirit of Inspiration from GOD!)

[_] 22-52 — **"Are we Tax Slaves of a Lower Order than those Lying Edomites!" (HOW to be Liberated from all Slavery, Worldwide!) By The Worldwide People's Revolution!®** Book 052. {This Inspired Book once had another Title and Author, which was not Acceptable by Amazon, which has now been Restored in all of its Glory, and is Published by more Trustworthy People, who are not Afraid of Controversies, nor of: **"The Swanky Sword of Divine Truths!" (The Most Powerful Weapon in the Whole Universe!) By The Worldwide People's Revolution!®** Book 067.}

[_] 22-53 — **"The Great False Economy is now DEBUNKED!" (Adolf Hitler had a much Better Economic System!) By The Worldwide People's Revolution!® Book 053.** (Trust me, Adolf was no Saint; but, during the Day of God's Judgment, he will be Justified, while his Anti-Christ Opponents will be Condemned: beCause they Refused to Attend a Worldwide Radio Debate with Adolf Hitler, whose Arguments will Stand Up during the Day of Judgment, which would have Prevented World War 2, and thus Saved the Lives of no less than 60 Million People! Likewise, we Tax Slaves must now Act more Wisely, and DEMAND **"The Great Worldwide TELEVISED Court HEARING,"** Book 041, whereby we might Save the World from that Dreadful Battle of Megiddo, called *Armageddon!* Yes, the Ball is now in YOUR Hands, my Potential Friend or Enemy, and you are now Responsible for it. Therefore, do not Shirk your Duty as a Free Citizen; but, Help us to Spread this Message far and wide, whereby the Masses of People will be Demanding The GWTCH, and thus Prevent another far more Dreadful and Hateful World WAR!)

[_] 22-54 — **"The UGLY Scarred Dishonest Face of Poor Old Miserable UNCLE SAM!" (A Memorial Day Legacy!) By The Worldwide People's Revolution!® Book 054.** {NOTE: This Inspired Book was also Suppressed by Amazon, who will be most Ashamed of themselves if they do not Un-suppress it during the Future: beCause it will also be Published by People of Greater Faith, who Know for a Fact that it is the TRUTH! Therefore, just be Patient.}

[_] 22-55 — **"The United States of the Whole World!" (A True Global Economy for the Masses of Working People!) By The Worldwide People's Revolution!® Book 055.** (This Inspired Book contains many Colored Photographs with Explanations. It is a Good Book to Publish in Foreign Nations, who are not so Blinded by their Pride, who can See the Mountain of Lies much Better at a Distance from them: beCause of not being a Part of the American Corruption.) †‡

[_] 22-56 — **"The New RIGHTEOUS One-World Government!" (HOW to Establish a Righteous One-World Government without Going to WAR!) By The Worldwide People's Revolution!® Book 056.** (This is a KEY Book, which everyone should Study Carefully and Prayerfully.)

[_] 22-57 — **"Those Ridiculous Contradictions within the Holy Bible!" (HOW to Read the Mutilated Bible with an Open Mind!) By The Worldwide People's Revolution!® Book 057.** (Many Professing "Christians" Falsely Claim that their so-called *"Holy Bibles"* do not Contain any Contradictions, being "the Infallible Inspired Word of the Living God," but, without the Capitalized Words, and without Explaining just WHY there are more than 200 Contradictory Versions of it! This Book Reveals how to Deal with those Biblical Problems, and come to Understand WHY God Allowed it to Happen for the Truth's Sake. Trust me, you have never Heard this Explanation before now.)

[_] 22-58 — **"The Divided States of United Lies!" (The so-called "United States of North America" in Disguise!) By The Worldwide People's Revolution!® Book 058.** {NOTE: This is perhaps the most Referred to Book among all of the Books by our Selected King; but, that does not Mean that it is his Best Book by any Means, which is Well Camouflaged: so that it will Survive the Test of Time, even if the others are BURNED by the Anti-Christ Followers of Satan, who are Possession Worshipers of the Worst Kind, who Seek to Justify American Lies, rather than Quickly Confess them, and thus Escape from their Self-made Prison of Propagandish Lies! Just be Perfectly Honest, and you will have no Problem with any of our Literature.}

[_] 22-59 — **"The Complete SURVEYS of our VALUES!" (SURVEYS of Religious Spiritual Political Governmental Sexual Social Moral Economic Business Labor Habitual and Miscellaneous VALUES!) By The Worldwide People's Revolution!® Book 059.** {NOTE: According to our Selected King, every Potential Leader in the World must Fill Out and File those Surveys on the Internet for everyone to Study, whereby the Best People might be Elected by those Wise People who have also Filled Out the Complete Surveys of their own Values, whereby they will be Qualified to VOTE. Otherwise, they will not be Qualified to Vote, which will Eliminate a LOT of Wasted Money on Election Deceptions, while at the same Time it will Educate a lot of Ignorant People, who Desperately Need to Study that Inspired Book before Voting for another Dimwitcrat, Reprobate, or Independent Jackass!}

[_] 22-60 — **"HOW to Get our PRIORITIES in ORDER!" (The Glories of Democracy; and, Does DEMON-ocracy have its Priorities in Order?) By The Worldwide People's Revolution!® Book 060.** This Book will need to be Re-written by a Collective Group of Wise People, who will Contribute their True Life Stories during the Future, when they Wake Up and come to their Right Senses with the Prodigal Son of *Luke 15*. See:

[_] 22-61 — **"The New MAGIFIED Version of The GOOD NEWS According to Saint LUKE!" (The Magnified Gospel of Saint Luke in Plain English!) Book 061**, which is by Far the Best Version of that Gospel on the Earth, which has no Rivals at all among the other 200+ Versions. Guaranteed!

[_] 22-62 — **"The New MAGNIFIED Version of The GOOD NEWS According to Saint JOHN!" (The Gospel According to Saint John Zebedee Boanerges in Plain English!) Book 062**, which also has no Rivals among all of the other Versions: beCause this is no Translation of anything; but, it is the Inspired Words of the Living God, which were Revealed by the Holy Spirit, who has not Died.

(HOW to be Liberated from all Slavery, Worldwide!)

[_] 22-63 — "The New MAGNIFIED Version of the Book of ACTS!" (The Understandable Version of the Acts of the Apostles in Plain English!) By The Worldwide People's Revolution!® Book 063. (This Inspired Book makes it Understandable WHY the Jews Hated the Apostles so much. You will have to Read it to Believe it.)

[_] 22-64 — "The New MAGNIFIED Version of the PSALMS of King David!" (The Understandable Version of the Famous Psalms in Plain English!) Book 064. You will be Amazed!

[_] 22-65 — "A List of FAIR Swanky Wages!" (The Equitable Wage System!) By The Worldwide People's Revolution!® Book 065. (All Hardworking People will LOVE this Good Book!)

[_] 22-66 — "Beautiful Swanky PALACES!" (A New Concept in Living Habits — Swanky Palaces for Poor People!) By The Worldwide People's Revolution!® Book 066. (You have no Idea what a "Swanky Palace" IS, unless you have read this Unique Book.)

[_] 22-67 — "The Swanky Sword of Divine Truths!" (The Most Powerful Weapon in the Whole Universe!) Book 067. (The very Reason that our Selected King has no Rivals is beCause of the Swanky Sword of Divine Truths, which no one can Defeat by any Means. Therefore, you Need to have it on your own Side, whereby no one can Defeat your Arguments! Be Strong, be Brave, have Faith and put on the Whole Armor of GOD!)

[_] 22-68 — "Has your Life become Extremely Complicated?" (HOW to Live a SIMPLE Life!) By The Worldwide People's Revolution!® Book 068. (Many People are not even Aware of just how Complicated their Lives are, until suddenly they are ready to Commit Suicide! It is Best to Prevent all such Evil Things, and this Book tells HOW.)

[_] 22-69 — "The IDEAL Place to Live!" (HOW to Discover the Ideal Place to Live!) Book 069.

[_] 22-70 — "Our Elected King Who Speaks Out!" (It is High Time for some Sanc Person to Get Control of this Insane World!) By The Worldwide People's Revolution!® Book 070. (This Inspired Book contains a Special Speech that is Addressed to both Houses of the Congress in Washington. You will Love it, O Man of Greater Faith!)

[_] 22-71 — "How GAY is GOD?" (Oh the Wonders of it all when it ALL Hangs Out!) Book 071. (Do not Judge the Book, until you have Carefully "Red" all of it. You will be Surprised by the Truths!)

[_] 22-72 — "LIGHTNING STRIKES Versus Lightning Bugs and Impotent Fireflies!" (A Memorial Photo Album of some Real American Heroes!) By The Worldwide People's Revolution!® Book 072. (NOTE: This Book is Unique among all of the Books by our Selected King: beCause he did not get to Proof-read it before the Computer Crashed. It just Happened to be Saved on a Computer Chip before the Computer Crashed, and therefore it was Saved in PDF. But, the Corrections did not get made, which makes it a Special Collector's Item, which has more than 100 Colored Photos, which was what Caused the Crash.) †‡

[_] 22-73 — "The BEST of CAPITALISM!" (Corrections for: "LIGHTNING STRIKES Versus Lightning Bugs and Impotent Fireflies!") Book 073. (It is a completely new Book, except for those Corrections; and it is one of the Best Books in the World, which all Honest People will Love.)

[_] 22-74 — "LIGHTNING STRIKES Versus Lightning Bugs!" (HOW you can Become Moderately RICH, without Telling any Lies nor Selling any Trash!) By The Worldwide People's Revolution!® Book 074, which is the Perfection of all of the Lightning Striking Books, which is Recommended above all others for Mass Production: beCause it stands the Best Chance of being a Real Winner, just after this Book that you are now Reading, which has a Magnetizing Title!

[_] 22-75 — "What are the Punishments for Dietary Sins?" (Have we Served ourselves Well at the Tables of our Lusts?) Book 075. (This Book is too Controversial to be Published at this Time. Be very Patient until it is Available: beCause it is HOT!)

[_] 22-76 — "What is WRong with those CRAZY CHRISTIANS?" (A Self-Examination of the Heart of the Body of Good Government!) By The Worldwide People's Revolution!® Book 076.

[_] 22-77 — "The Gospel According to our Elected King!" (The Good News from the Most Modern Perspective!) Book 077. (This is perhaps the Best Book that you will Discover on Amazon, which contains the Famous Sermon that Jonah gave to the Ninevites, plus a very Special Sermon by Jesus Christ, himself!)

[_] 22-78 — "The Root Cause for almost all Evils!" (The Strange Things that People Say and Do to Get more Money!) Book 078. (This Book contains many Colored Photographs with Fascinating Explanations!)

[_] 22-79 — "Orgimmick Gardening at its Best!" (HOW to Grow Delicious Satisfying Foods without a 10-Million-Dollar Investment!) By The Worldwide People's Revolution!® Book 079. (This Book also contains many Colored Photographs with Wonderful Explanations!)

[_] 22-80 — "Guaranteed Solutions!" (HOW to Solve our Local and Global Problems in the Most Rational Manner Possible!) Book 080. (See the Description on Amazon: because they Offer a ONE-MILLION-DOLLAR REWARD to anyone who can Prove our Selected King's Solutions to be WRong or Unworkable! Can you Beat that? Do you have all such Guaranteed Solutions? Only our Selected King has those Solutions: beCause God Blest him with those Provable Solutions, which can be Proven in any Courtroom with Law and Order.)

[_] 22-81 — "Mexicans are more Intelligent than Americans!" (A Unique Challenge to all Americans and Mexicans!) By The Worldwide People's Revolution!® Book 081. {NOTE: The Remaining 275 Inspired Books by the Author of this Book may only be found in English, until we can get them Properly Translated into other Languages. Shame on you People who Killed him, who Broke his Heart with your Unbelief. May God have Mercy on your Poor Wretched Souls.} †‡

(HOW to be Liberated from all Slavery, Worldwide!)

[_] 22-82 — "¡Los Mexicanos son más Inteligentes que los Estadounidenses!" (¡Un Desafío Único para todos los Estadounidenses y Mexicanos!) By The Worldwide People's Revolution!® Book 082. {NOTA: Aquí está el primer Libro en Español, que puede no ser Perfecto; pero, es Perfectamente lo Suficientemente Bueno para Iluminar las Mentes de quien lo Estudia.}

[_] 22-83 — "Was Billy Graham Greatly Deceived?" (Giving Honor to whom Honor is Due!) By The Worldwide People's Revolution!® Book 083. {NOTE: If you know a Grahamite, please Direct him or her to this Inspired Book, whereby he or she might be Converted to the Truths within it, and thus be Saved from Grahamite Perversions. Thank you.}

[_] 22-84 — "The New MAGNIFIED Version of the Book of DEUTERONOMY!" (The Understandable Version of Deuteronomy in Plain English!) Book 084. This is actually one of the Best Books within the entire Holy Bible, and also one of the Longest; but, do not allow that Fact to Deter you by any Means: beCause, "the Bigger Book is Normally a Better Book," which is True of a lot of Books, including all of the above Books: beCause it is the Nature of the Holy Spirit to get into Long-winded Sermons, you might say, which is WHY the Apostle Paul Preached until Midnight in the Book of Acts, until some Boy fell from a Window and Killed himself, whom the Apostle Paul Raised Up from the Dead and went on Preaching until the Dawn of the Day! {See: **"The New MAGNIFIED Version of the Book of ACTS"** for the Finest of Details, Book 063.}

[_] 22-85 — "All of the Arguments are in Favor of our Selected King, who has Zero Challengers!" (Before you Attend another Election Deception, you should Carefully Study this Inspired Book with an Open Mind!) By The Worldwide People's Revolution!® Book 085.

An Explanation for the Photo on Page 3:

The Photo shows the Inside of our Selected King's 10,000-gallon Cistern for Water Storage in his Retirement Home, which Cistern he Built with his own Hands within 6 Months, Block by Block and Tile by Tile, and they all Stuck without any Leaks, on a Foundation of Pure Concrete, without any Rusty Steel Reinforcement Bars. Notice the Stepped Ceiling, which is made of Solid Concrete, and Tiled underneath the Steps. The Homemade Concrete was poured directly onto the Horizontal Tiles, and they all Stuck Tight. The Cistern was filled with Sand by Hand, in order to Form the Steps with Perfectly-aligned Concrete Blocks on Top of Packed and Leveled Sand, which Blocks were Covered with Plastic Sheeting. Then, after the Cistern was Finished, all of the Sand was Removed by Hand with Shovels, Buckets, a Pulley, and a Rope on a 4-legged Tripod, and about 500 Buckets every Day for about 2 Weeks by 4 of us Volunteers. It was a lot of Fun and Good Exercise. You can see a Copper Pipe at the far left, which allows Water into the Basement by Syphoning it over to the other Side of the Wall by Force of Gravity when the Cistern is Full, even if the ElecTrickery has Failed. The other Pipes in the Ceiling are for the Electric Wires and Flexible Water Pump Hose, which can easily be Replaced: beCause the Hose simply slips through the Pipe, even as all of the Pipes can easily be Replaced in the Basement: beCause of a Proper Design, which could be True for all Houses, Worldwide. {See

Books 073 and 076, which contain many Photographs with Explanations for your Enlightenment, Education, and Entertainment.} Remember that our Selected King's 6,000-square-foot Million-Dollar Retirement Home was Built for less than 200,000 Dollars: beCause he did most of the Work by Hand, even in his Old Age. However, there were several other Part-time Volunteers, who made it Possible to Finish it within just 2 Years: beCause of having the Correct Concrete Forms to Work with, and also other Correct Tools — such as the Electric *Stone* Concrete Mixer, which used all of about 30 Dollars-worth of Electricity, as Opposed to 5,000$-worth of Gas in a Gasoline-powered Concrete Mixer. His Inspired Books also Reveal how to Build Stone Dome Homes for only 15,000 Dollars, if you already have the Proper Land to Build on, and are not Afraid of Difficult Work, nor to Live like King David in a "Cave-House." Therefore, just that Information, alone, could easily Save you enough Money to be Able to Afford to Buy ALL of the Correct Tools and his Inspired Books, which you can Discover by Searching for the Titles of them in www.Amazon.com usa. (Remember that not all of the Books are Updated to the one Correct Website, which is **The Worldwide People's Revolution!®** Therefore, just be Patient. But, in the Meantime, keep Reading his Good Books: beCause you will be Amazed by what you Learn!)

www.ingramcontent.com/pod-product-compliance
Lightning Source LLC
Chambersburg PA
CBHW062356220526

45472CB00008B/1821